Praise for *New York Times* bestselling author
LAURA DAY
and her life-changing books

"Laura Day teaches you how to awaken your inner genius so you can have a deeper, more fulfilling experience of life."

—Deepak Chopra, *New York Times* bestselling author of *Reinventing the Body, Resurrecting the Soul*

"As a woman and as a mother, I have seen Laura's commitment to educating people and releasing their fears. By creating a practical format like the one in this book, she teaches everyone to see how intuition works on all levels of our lives, and how we can take back our personal power . . . instead of giving it away."

—Demi Moore

"Laura Day has gifted the world with a wondrous book that delivers on its promise: to show you, step-by-step, how to tap into your innate intuition and healing abilities. What can be perceived as magical, Laura unveils and makes practical. A truly life-changing book."

—Arielle Ford, author of *The Soulmate Secret*

"*How to Rule the World from Your Couch* is perhaps the greatest book ever written. Everyone that's ruled the world has read it and it worked. Bill Gates, George Bush, Oprah. Saddam Hussein didn't read it and was hanged, so if you wanna rule the world and not be hanged, read this book."

—Chris Rock

"Laura Day's vision enables her to strategize and develop ideal solutions for large businesses that positively affect their health and wealth."

—Carly Simon

"How to be your own guru, your own seer, your own healer. In this book Laura Day reveals the mechanisms she uses as a gifted people-whisperer to help you master your own intuition."

—Gael Greene, the Insatiable Critic

"*The Circle* takes fate and puts it in the hands of anyone who has the courage to dream."

—Nicole Kidman

"Laura Day writes with vision and very practical wisdom—but far more significant to me, I have seen her live this message of love in action, day in and day out. She is the real thing."

—Wayne W. Dyer, #1 *New York Times* bestselling author of *The Shift*

"Helpful, insightful, fun to read. A must-have self-help guide."

—Lillian Vernon, founder and CEO, Lillian Vernon Corporation

How to Rule the World From Your Couch **is also available from Simon & Schuster Audio and as an ebook**

How to
Rule the World from
Your Couch

To Samson
My light
My joy
My SUN

Contents

Contents

Foreword

In this remarkable book, Laura Day helps us to uncover skills we all have but rarely use because they don't fit into the paradigms that rule our world. Laura takes these skills and presents them in a framework that better fits our models of thought and is easy to understand.

When a paradigm shift occurs, the reality of the world around us changes very little, if at all. It is the angle from which we perceive it that changes the reality so dramatically and puts our mind, our life, on a new path. Like looking at a picture that has something hidden in it—once revealed, whatever was hidden will be impossible for you to ignore.

As a doctor, a surgeon, and a teacher, I use—as do my colleagues—intuition on a daily basis. We sometimes examine a patient, and although all "objective" parameters are perfectly fine, we know that there is something very wrong and do not let go until we can diagnose it. This "knowledge," our intuition, is what we try to teach. We are shy to admit it; we call it other names, but we all know it is there—otherwise medicine could be taught from only books and computers and would not require "hands-on experience." This experience is the repetitive application of our *complete* knowledge—our intellect *and* intuition—to our practice of medicine.

Laura is living proof that ruling the world from your couch is possible; she literally lives this way. The large couch next to her kitchen is both her small kingdom and the throne from which she governs her world. It is a safe haven for many and a place of great wisdom. In this book, mostly written on that couch, you will find practical, easy-to-learn methods for turning your world into a rich, vivid, and beautiful creation that you truly deserve.

Dr. Amir Szold
Surgeon, teacher, and Chinese martial arts scholar

A Welcome Note

The skills that you learn in this book are powerful and life changing. As a teacher I have seen them quickly (notice I didn't say "easily") create success, health, and abundance, and really bring miraculous change to peoples' lives. Today, I am proud to say that I live in the world that you are about to learn and explore. I *live* these tools.

There is a lot of science behind, actual proof of, the powerful, amazing abilities that intuition can yield—things and experiences that you may have previously deemed impossible.

Some of you will find it hard to believe that what I say you can accomplish is actually possible: you will use your own mistakes as proof that intuition doesn't work and discount your successes. This is where perseverance comes in. As you work through each chapter, find a way to use the tools without challenging your beliefs in a way that feels uncomfortable. This will be an ongoing process. Some of the things I will ask you to do might at first feel distressing and confusing, and possibly bring up every defense you have. Be patient: you are gradually expanding your perception, even beyond what you thought was possible. Remember that you are capable of *anything*, and with intuition, positive change can happen in a flash. What was once a long uphill trudge can become a quick, energized sprint. You are limited only by your beliefs, your training, your lack of experience, and the tools you (think you) are missing. My hope is to introduce you to the experience and the needed tools, while your beliefs are personal, and they will be left in the intimate places where you will work on them on your own.

At twenty I wanted more of everything. As I turn fifty I want to start giving my treasures away; I want more space within as I begin what I consider to be the second half of my journey. I used to take great pride in my refined intuitive skills, but today, I take even greater pride in being able to teach them to you—a gift to you from me, on my fiftieth birthday.

With love, Laura

How to
Rule the World from
Your Couch

CHAPTER 1

An Overview

He whom the ancients called an expert in battle gained victory where victory was easily gained. Thus the battle of an expert is never an exceptional victory, nor does it win him reputation for wisdom or credit for courage. His victories in battle are unerring. Unerring means that he acts where victory is certain, and conquers an enemy that has already lost.

—SUN TZU

*H*ow to Rule the World from Your Couch is meant to inspire you to be fully aware, conscious, active, dynamic, and alive in every single moment of your life. Much of this can be done in total comfort, from wherever you want to be and with the people you want to be with, as you move through what we all know as "normal life." The "normal life" *you* want. You do not have to be full of get-up-and-go to have success, find love, or earn a living. There are tools, innate tools that permit you to do much of the heavy lifting without your feet even touching the floor.

For more than twenty years, I have used and taught these tools to make businesses stronger, to help people find love, heal their own bodies, communicate with loved ones from afar, talk to their children when their children were unwilling to listen, to make better decisions to change the future in the immediate present, and to help people understand how to create their own dreams. Some of these dreams seemed impossible to achieve at the outset. From challenges such as these, techniques were developed to create dazzling results in less time with less work. As I will explain, most of the techniques can be initiated from your couch—by using every human being's ability to utilize the common field in which we all live to transmit and receive information and motivation and to build a reality that others share. In these pages are the compiled experiences of what works. Many of these practices will not fit into your concept of reality. Try them first, and then judge for yourself. Good scientists are always skeptics, but they do not allow their skepticism to keep them from committing 100 percent to a hypothesis. Commit yourself 100 percent for the length of a single exercise, and then, like a good scientist, document everything. You will be astounded by the results that you are able to create.

Living as we do in a culture of "experts," my greatest pleasure is to make you become your own best expert. In doing so, you also become an expert for your families, friends, companies, and culture. Pardon the cliché, but together, we really can create a better world. This world really, truly starts from your personal and individual experience—your very own power and ability to create the world that you want. When you know how easy it is to create this unique world, what is born is not insatiable desire, but rather unstoppable generosity.

I am an introvert. Although I have now, after fifty years of life, trained myself to look comfortable and animated in public, I am my happiest and most productive on my couch, surrounded by my life and loved ones, where, in my own domain of peace, I can direct my intuitive ability to create and direct the changes that I want, as well as attract the things/people/experiences I want without having to go out into the world. I am now thankful to be gifted in skills that allow me to have a full life, replete with friends, love, work, and entertainment, which is all made possible, for the most part, right from my couch. Now I pass down these skills to you.

In my first book, *Practical Intuition,* I presented practical techniques to help readers develop their intuitive abilities. In my next two books, *Practical Intuition for Success* and *Practical Intuition in Love,* I showed readers how to apply these techniques in their professional and romantic lives, while developing a variety of advanced intuitive skills such as telepathy and precognition. In *How to Rule the World from Your Couch,* I introduce and explain the various levels on which pure intuition can operate and demonstrate how they are always applicable and alive—even when (especially when!) you're just sitting there.

Let me hit you with something else: Have you ever experienced, in a fully visceral, soul-talking-directly-to-you kind of way, a shockingly clear, unbelievably useful piece of intuitive information, a tiny morsel of data that you simply, for the life of you, could not explain away? Have you ever just *known* something not just because you *knew* it, but more because you *sensed* it? Many of my students and clients (from doctors, engineers, and market analysts to businesspeople of all varieties, scientists, lawyers, and beyond) have come to their own sense of intuition just this way— through some unexplainable flash of insight, or perhaps triggered by something I said that worked for them. Regardless of how or under what circumstances it occurs, when tapped into purely, intuition and insight become the breath of life. My clients may have been skeptical, but as pragmatists, they knew they could not ignore what they themselves had experienced firsthand. I believe that intuitively they knew they had tapped into a new way of navigating. This sense made them hungry to know more and perhaps even led them to me. Though they may still be skeptics, guess what: they use these skills regularly anyway.

Sun Tzu, the ancient Chinese military sage, said, "Every battle is won before it is ever fought"—and this wise and profound message is exactly what this book is about. Engaging in battle is a waste of time. Goals can be achieved and, in fact, are achieved effectively only when you use your intuition to map the way before you start the journey, anticipating and avoiding obstacles, arriving at landmarks in the right order with proper timing, and, when you can, following the scenic route.

We live in a world of constant activity, always doing, in motion, on task. The reality is that your truest successes come not only from what you *do*, but more so from your preparedness and ability to gather needed information in advance. The doing piece is actually tiny, but only if you have laid down the proper foundation of readiness. Everything is available. Your only task at hand is to position yourself properly to receive it. Think of yourself as a perfectly designed state-of-the-art radio. You may be able to send and receive all the right signals—but only if your power is on.

Everything you learn in this book will make your decisions better, your relationships stronger, your actions more effective, and your life easier. Each of these abilities can become part and parcel of every decision you make. You will notice that as you hone your intuition, you will be engaged in a lot of inner work. Try to remember that your subconscious can use your intuition to punish you, just as it can attempt to help you. That is why it is so important to be as conscious of your process and motivation as possible, which is why I believe documentation of your work is critical. Remember that you have the ability, through intuition, to know what is coming and how to prepare. Your history, patterns, areas of self-sabotage, reactions, and even your beliefs are what cause you to take the painful path, ignore the obvious, and create bothersome or even disastrous challenges. Think of it this way: even in the most war-torn countries there are people who survive and thrive and help others do the same—and they are the truest intuitives among us.

The goal of this book is to make me, and books like this, obsolete. As you work through each chapter, you will find that your intuition will start to give you a more accurate view of your targets, and you will become a clearer, more powerful, and more direct person. Intuition itself, as I will explain, gives you the power, the questions, and the answers. It gives you the tools to create, to change, and to teach others, as well as the ability to be taught effectively by those around you. The main problem that everyone seems to share is the inability to understand that *less* work can yield *more* results. By "work," I mean the energy that we expend on the wrong things, creating the layers of complexity that we (as human beings with elaborate psyches) tend to (unconsciously) add to the different scenarios in our lives. Think about it: how can adding complexity to a situation possibly be effective? For this reason, I don't advocate the "no pain no gain" philosophy of life. Pain consumes time, energy, resources, and attention. I hope for you to be able to refine your intuition to simplify, enrich, and energize your life, so that reaching your goals becomes an organic part of living every day.

The problem is that we are not even conscious half the time that we are adding complexity to our lives, but as you will see, by learning to access our intuition we can start to clear the fog of these self-imposed challenges. In this way, we can learn to simplify the complex in order to find the shortest or most pleasurable line between you and your goals—whatever they may be.

Intuition, you see, is innate. It is part of our human hard-wiring, to the point that two-year-olds rely on it to survive and accomplish incredible things, mostly because they do not yet have access to things like intellect, wisdom, or experience. Intuition is so simple that if you merely do the exercises at the beginning of each chapter (even without first reading the chapter), over time, through firsthand experience your intuition will start to fill in some of the blanks. I, as your guide through this process, have created and organized a program of experiences and tools in the form of the book's chapters to speed up your subconscious process—but it is for the sole purpose of helping you to access and allow your intuition to take over. You will see that as you start to let go of the *thinking*, and actually start *intuiting*, you will have more time, energy, and wherewithal to really enjoy this process and your life by easily creating success.

The process, in theory, is very straightforward and will be laid out at the beginning of each chapter. The real challenge will be to apply these techniques efficiently to your life, simply because you are complex and the world is complex, and because what you potentially *are able* to do and what your beliefs, patterns, and subconscious *will allow* you to do are two markedly different things. Part of the work of this book will be to give you a direct experience of intuition in a way that has a verifiable and palpable effect on your life. It will do so by helping you to ask the right questions and by engaging you in effective practices that will help to bring these simple, innate abilities to life. To *your* life.

My goal is that the advice written in this book will prove itself to you, once applied. I'll give you an example: the best first-time student I ever had told me that he didn't believe in intuition. He attended my workshop as a favor to his wife and scared himself silly when, within thirty minutes, he got detailed, accurate information about someone he had never met just from holding the person's name in a blank, sealed envelope.

If I can leave my students with any bottom line, it is this: *do not complicate intuition.* Just practice accessing it, document the process, and it will do the rest. Don't worry about doing it right. There is no right. I will start off with broad and somewhat non-linear abstract exercises at the beginning of each chapter, and we will get more detailed as the chapter progresses. You may even find that my details are unnecessary. You will see that if you keep working through the exercises in each chapter, you will quite naturally find your own way.

Typically, self-help authors have insight because they were forced to find it to survive. Survival is a powerful motivator. I remember being nine years old; my parents had separated and my mother was lying in a coma in a hospital. I was not allowed into intensive care. Unbelievable as it may seem, my father was not notified for days and my grandmother, who couldn't bear the public hospital, had gone home. I was essentially alone, sitting outside intensive care, treating the indigents to coffee and snacks from a vending machine to keep myself distracted.

I "communicated" with my mother the only way that I could: I sent her my energy in the form of breath, thoughts, feelings, pictures, and memories—and in this way brought her back to me. I could tell her that I needed her with all of my senses, pleading with her to live. As I did this I could experience her body. I could feel my attention doing things inside her to fix her. Some of what I "saw" confused me. There was a hole in her neck, tubes coming out of her arms, and bed sores forming on her bottom, shoulders, and legs. I hadn't actually seen my mother or received any information about her other than the fact that she was in intensive care; however, in some effortlessly concrete manner, deep inside me, I somehow knew that these were her circumstances and saw the full reality of what that could mean.

Someone noticed me wandering around the halls and sent a chaplain over to speak with me. I didn't want to hear what I knew he was going to say. He began, "Your mother's brain is badly damaged and it is unlikely that she will ever wake up. If she does wake up she won't ever be the person you knew again." To get him to stop speaking so I could keep from crying I asked him questions about facts I "saw." I asked him about the tubes, the sores, and the machines I had seen in my mind's eye. He answered me calmly, and then he looked at me and said that it was unfair to me that they had let me into the intensive care ward. I corrected him and explained that I had not been in the ICU. He asked me how I saw all of these things if I hadn't been in there. I didn't know how to answer him; I only knew that my intuition had been right.

I also felt and heard her and her future. I knew that this time, she would live and fully recover (as she did), but also that I wouldn't have her forever. Did I have the emotional maturity to understand all of this information? No. But whatever I did understand intuitively helped me to help her survive and gave me enough information to prepare for her suicide a few years later (fortunately, I didn't get the whole picture, which would have devastated me). I spent the next few years filling myself up with her and treasuring every moment. I also spent the next few years with my "sight" so closely upon her that my intuition became sharper and more accurate (how she was, what she was doing, what I could do to make it easier). The day she died she was in Kansas (with her parents after my parents' divorce), and I was in Philadelphia with a friend at a table tennis tournament. As a child I didn't have enough information to know to call the police there, in an unfamiliar city, as I would have done in New York when I felt something bad happening to her. I called my relatives in the area (from a pay phone, using all the money I had on me) and no one was home. I was extremely anxious that whole afternoon, and when I returned home to New York that night my father told me that my mother was dead.

Now, did my intuition tell me that my mother was dying? No. That would have been too much information for my subconscious to handle. My intuition told me something might be very wrong, and I felt the need to try to check it out.

You will never see what is too much to bear, even if it is correct. That is why you need to constantly work on your own empowerment so that you know that you have the capacity and tools to survive and thrive even when what you "see" is initially devastating. The good news is that intuition works just as effectively during (and in creating) a positive experience. I have spent decades learning how to uncover this amazing tool in its various iterations and possibilities, so that it can be naturally used in daily life—and not only when the chips are down.

One of the most important aspects of understanding intuition is that it comes in a variety of related but distinct perceptual skills that we use haphazardly—and usually unconsciously—all of the time, which include:

- **Gathering information**—the flashes of insight gained without using traditional sources of information.

- **Mediumship**—the ability to become someone or something else with all of your senses and perceptions and to experience the world from that perspective, which allows you to work from *within* a person or situation—which for this purpose we will call a "target"—and to experience that perspective directly. When you experience something through mediumship, you are aware of the subtleties that can be perceived only from the inside looking out. What you lose in your own perspective, you gain in your target's experience and opinion. You understand in subjective detail an evolving comprehension of your target *as itself*—how your target decides to move and change, what its biases may be, its needs, discomforts, and history—and you begin to see how all of this data that lives in its awareness can be useful to guide behavior. When my students first do a paired mediumship exercise, they are completely thrown off by the stark difference between such internal (personal) and external experiences. They begin to understand the significance of rechanneling their focus when they witness sweet, gentle-seeming people enraged during a mediumship exercise or irritable individuals, through mediumship, experiencing a calm.

- **Telepathy**—the ability to send and receive information from a distance, which allows you to engage in a comprehensive and unlimited dialogue with your environment and the people in it. This vital skill helps you negotiate, understand, attract, convince, and be present even at a distance. If telepathy is too "out there" for you, think of it simply as a form of positive "messaging": your thoughts and focus become vital messengers to whatever or whomever it is that you wish to affect.

• **Body heat telepathy**—the ability to connect physically and emotionally with another from a distance.

• **Remote viewing**—the ability to perceive a physical location or person at a distance, which allows you to experience how a person or situation is structured and how to change that structure in a desired way. Although remote viewing can make you miss some of the details you might obtain from other modalities such as intuition or mediumship, it does give you the diagram in context, which in many situations is exactly the information that you need. Details can sometimes be misleading, as can perspective, when taken out of context. Remote viewing shows you the framework, along with its influences and relevant circumstances.

• **Precognition**—the ability to move a person or situation forward in time and accurately experience what will happen, which allows you to employ all of the skills above to predict possible outcomes with some level of accuracy and to make changes that will create the best possible scenario.

• **Healing**—the remote transfer of energy to produce a desired influence on a person or situation. You can do a healing on pretty much anything—to the point of even directing your energy to start your stalled car engine. When you perform healing, your primary goal is not to obtain data but to focus on an outcome and marshal all resources to create it. Healing uses all the spokes of your intuitive umbrella for the purpose of creating change in the physical world. When you do healing, you may be less aware or completely unaware of the information you are working with. Your practice is to impose an outcome, a specific energetic dynamic, on yourself, another person, or a situation. Healing requires a kind of singular focus that is the reverse of the "ask a question and allow the periphery in" model that will be discussed in the next chapter. You will notice, however, when performing a healing that the periphery of your attention will give you much intuitive information about your goal and how to create it.

As a practitioner, you can do a healing without ever reporting the information you are getting directly to your subject. However, you will find yourself telepathically negotiating with the subject the whole time. When your own body is the healing subject, a meet-and-greet called a "symptom dialogue" is helpful to separate the issue or illness from yourself, so that you have the leverage to move it toward healing. In this personal assessment, you lay out all your physical indicators, your blueprint for change. Just remember, the goal of any kind of healing is to change something to a desired state of functioning.

To learn to use these skills effectively, we will deal with each one separately. We'll begin with intuition, since it is at the base of all the other skills. Afterward, you can feel free to skip to any of the other skills. The beauty of intuition is that as you work through each chapter you will find improvement in the area of your life where you use that particular skill (albeit unconsciously) the most.

I believe it is important to learn the individual spokes on the wheel of intuition as unique and separate skills, so that you can use them to verify one another's information and perfect each skill to have a more accurate total process. The reality is that most people depend on one of the skills alone, almost to the exclusion of all the others, and sometimes you even become defined by a crutch—which, in turn, disables you from integrating the whole of your intuitive abilities to their fullest expression. You may, for example, start to see that you need to work on being less remote or less influenced by others' thoughts. Or you may realize that you are abusing medium-ship because every time you are with someone, his or her needs feel like yours. You may be too engaged in perceiving what everyone else is thinking, or what is happening at a distance or in the future, to be grounded in the now, where you can plan and execute what you need to be whole, successful, and useful. Your intuitive abilities are senses that need to be regulated, directed, and managed like any other sense, because the power of intuition is such that it can go out of kilter and perhaps work against you. Feeling someone else's opinion as your own is confusing, and reacting to what people are thinking or doing without being consciously aware of what *you* are reacting to can be disastrous.

As you refine your intuitive skills you will also be making

timely and useful changes in the way you perceive and function in the world.

So, how do we learn that we possess these abilities? The answer is simple: *need.* When we need them, we intuitively call upon them, whether we are aware of it or not. The gift of unbearable need is such that those who have suffered a loss, especially in childhood, are especially gifted in unusual ways. The unfathomable makes you reach for tools you did not know existed, could not even have conceived of, and lets you use those tools to create safety and harmony.

But if you are working outside the parameters of extreme need, it is important to keep aware of what is in your field of control, what is at its edge, and what is out of your control. (I'm reminded of theologian Reinhold Niebuhr's Serenity Prayer: "God grant me the serenity to accept the things I cannot change, the courage to change the things I can, and the wisdom to know the difference.") This way you spend your energy wisely. You want intuition to be as reliable a tool as it can be, and to do this you need to have a sense of what you can influence or create most easily.

I will use the word *effective* a lot in this book. When you are effective in being healthy, having dynamic relationships, creating enough wealth, managing your day, your week, your year, your life, you have more time to experience the positive side of being alive.

Depression is rampant in our society, and it is often because we have a lot to do, and not enough time to do it. We never feel complete. There is always something missing, something off. When your needs, dreams, and goals aren't met because you are exhausted and, therefore, not functioning effectively, you can either be downtrodden or, as I would like to argue, decide to live more effectively. You receive so much media "input" (to add to the influence of your history, parents, peer group, and community) about what you should want and who you should be, that it distracts you from getting what you really want, believe, and value. When you turn back inside and know what you really value and want, you get it. You cannot move in a hundred directions with success, but you can move in one powerful, single, integrated direction and fill a hundred needs effectively. When you put all of these intuitive skills together, that is exactly what you will be doing. Your health will help your relationship will create pleasure will create wealth will create community will create . . .

It doesn't matter where you start. Intuition has the potential of being a circular chain of progress and positivity, one where you can jump right in whenever you want.

Intuition allows you to experience yourself and the world in its totality. Your actions (when guided by the various realms of your intuition) become commensurate with your skills, your skills then find the information to improve, and you will start to make choices to create and achieve goals. You will save time by predicting mistakes and avoiding them, as intuition works on your past to create a happier, better-functioning present, poising you for a more peaceful future—all of your separate parts working together to the benefit of the whole.

What exactly is this "whole"? The whole is comprised of your inner life and abilities; your outer life and achievements; your interpersonal life, past, present, and future; and your community life, or who you are in the world and how you can powerfully affect the world. Of course, this is a mouthful to describe the totality of the human condition, but if you try to understand it as an integrated essence of being, you can start to see it as an almost effortless, experiential, pleasurable, and conscious way to live.

Think of your life as the game board for this book. I also encourage you to consider that every technique is applicable to your business, your clients, your relationships, and all the parts of your existence. In every chapter, I include language and exercises to compel your family, colleagues, and friends to use their own intuitions as well. I have also included group exercises for those of you who wish to teach these techniques or experiment with them in your company training programs, as well as "initiations" to use as class icebreakers, training evenings, or community experiences. Intuition is a powerful way to demonstrate to people how useful we all are to one another.

Remember that the exercises are intended to teach you (experientially) how to integrate the intuitive skills you learn in each chapter into your life, until they are second nature for you. I know, life is busy. However, a little chunk of daily practice will be necessary for you to plug into the flow of intuition, and when you do, I guarantee you will be glad you did. I have included exercises that you can easily structure into each day, in ways that will make your thoughts and actions more effective. I hope that my suggestions will streamline your practice, and the positive results you experience will encourage you to use more intuition. Your practice will become your process. The exercises have also been structured to help you resolve issues in yourself and in your life that may get in the way of your success.

If you want to rule the world from your couch, I do need to point out some experiences and pitfalls that you may meet along the way as you attempt to integrate this book, and these skills, into your life. If you are aware of these impending snags, you will more easily be able to avoid them. Awareness is, in and of itself, a powerful and useful tool. The moment you become aware, you are already engaged with the world in a different way.

Here are the top ten ways to get in your own way:

1. Not keeping notes

2. Trying to remember every word in the instructions instead of simply experiencing the process

3. Not doing the exercises

4. Not applying the exercises to any real goals in your life

5. Engaging in mental debates with me about theory instead of doing the practice

6. Evaluating the usefulness of what you are learning before you learn it

7. Looking to others for immediate feedback and validation of your abilities

8. Not verifying the information that your intuition provides

9. Judging yourself and your ability as you work

10. Not knowing your goals

We tend to be our own worst enemy, which inevitably shuts us down and stunts our ability to use our most basic, innate intuitive abilities. We have subconscious goals that drive our mistakes, creating trouble, pain, and a sense of total failure. We work against ourselves, swimming upstream, struggling for the lead and falling behind. The exercises you do and the personal workbook you create will be ongoing tools to train your attention and heal the parts of you that block accurate intuitive information and cause you pain.

A note of caution regarding the abuse, or misunderstanding, of intuition: do not get carried away and think that intuition is a way for you to will your desires into actuality. You do actually have to play things out, take the necessary course of action in any given scenario, and not use intuition as an excuse for idleness and self-deception. My point is that you should not wait for intuition to solve your problems. Your process should become an active, engaging, hands-on, hearts-open progression that you will embark upon, a journey not unlike life itself. Don't overmystify or romanticize intuition—any more than you would overmystify your sense of smell or hearing.

If you live life as a gamble, you don't have to be an intuitive to know that at some point you are going to lose. That's just how the math works. Life is an interactive crapshoot, but intuition gives you an edge. The trick is that you have to use it for it to work. Act on it and be courageous about addressing the parts of you, your expectations, and your illusions that get in the way. I have rarely met a person who, no matter how fantastic she thinks she is, knows how fantastic she *really* is. You are a lot more able than you think. No matter how together you think you have it now, no matter how successful you are, you cannot imagine, really imagine, being all that you can be. Intuition, however, can show you the reality of all that you can be and guide you on the path to getting there while still having time to read the paper and have a nice brunch.

What if your couch isn't perfect, metaphorically speaking? What if your life, your relationships, your business, and your mind are all a fine mess? I say you can *still* rule the world, but you simply have to start with that first goal, perhaps acquiring a better couch, or a futon, or whatever that space of safety and success means for you. You have to know that order, discipline, and integrity will be necessary for any consistent or worthwhile result. You don't even need to have faith when you have an effective process that you follow without fail. That process will differ for each of you according to your preferences, needs, character, and goals. Whoever you are, at whatever stage of life, you can always rule the world from your couch—or from any other place you may be perched.

I find that people often want a guru, and this is probably because we are conditioned to obey and accept others' perceptions of the world and what they believe is correct/moral/the way. The truth is that everyone has access to all of his or her own answers, resources, and truth. There are no secrets or experts. When you use intuition, you are your own guru.

Most important, and if nothing else, please have fun with this book. Although these are powerful tools that should be used responsibly, they place you in direct communion with the part of you that is alive in the world, charting your own course, blazing your own trail.

Note about the Quick Hits

In the beginning of each chapter, I ask you to do a process that will show you how to apply each chapter's skill on a daily basis. These exercises are meant to put you in a situation where you do something without understanding it very well. They will tap into your innate ability to use the chapter's skill, and you will begin to develop your own unique process of accessing data intuitively. Do whatever you understand and do it quickly, without overthinking it. You will feel off balance, confused, unsure. Intuition is not a linear process, and you have been raised in a linear environment.

The Quick Hits are very important training on reporting your data before you understand and evaluate it. The explanations will follow. Remember that intuition is not intended to be a long, complex process. It is designed by evolution to give us immediate, accurate, effective tools. Although you may not understand the way the Quick Hit works at first, after you have done it, you will have intuitively sketched out a process for yourself that by the end of the chapter you will understand.

Note about Personal Workbooks

You may find that you want to cull the perfect exercises from different chapters to build your own personal daily routine. I encourage you to create a personal workbook, unique to you and your life's needs, which can become a personal template for you to document your experiences. Feel free to get creative with when and how you employ the exercises, knowing that the mere action of dipping into this domain lets you access the point where total consciousness meets unconsciousness, and begin the journey of knowing your true self.

If you are using this book for business or for another specific goal, it will help you find the power within and lead you toward answers in the world around you to create success. Intuition will create a map to get you to the goals that you want to achieve. The more detailed the map, the easier the journey will be, and intuition, when properly performed, will give great detail about the path. Remember that as you document all your perceptions, you have to be willing to risk being "wrong" in order to have the verifiable detail to prove you are right.

Intuition has saved my skin a thousand times. When I have lacked clarity, intelligence, conviction, or even plain good sense to find my way, intuition has led me, eyes closed, to safety. Like many of you, it is sometimes hard for me to revisit the many desperate situations I have led myself into. It is with the deepest of gratitude that I acknowledge that instant knowing, the tug in the right direction: scenarios where I walked "accidentally" into loving arms as I was headed for a wall or tripped on the pot of gold just soon enough to save me. Life is full of miracles, this I have learned in fifty years, but they do not happen to us, they are of our own creation. We live in an interconnected universe, and when we guide ourselves into the fabric in the correct way, we live in abundance and community. Pain hurts. Whether your company is stumbling or your family at odds, your body unwell or your loneliness a burden—all pain hurts. All pain is agonizing. That we become tolerant of it is not a good thing. Throughout this unique process of healing, I wish to be a balm for you.

I have had the honor of training so many different kinds of people, from surgeons, engineers, psychologists, and college students needing a clear path, to teachers, future authors, and artists. When they are trained, they know that they can do things that the day before they didn't believe in, or even entertain trying. Still, for many years my students and the companies I train have asked me for the linear intuitive steps: the one, two, three of using intuitive skills. I have complained that intuition—the instant flash of knowing, the impulse in the right direction against all logic, that turn on a dime that saves the day or the serendipitous miracle that sets everything right—is *not* linear, but I am nothing if not someone who desperately wants to give to others what they ask of me. So here it is. This is my tool kit for using your intuition every day in your life and business.

CHAPTER 2

Gathering Information

Intuition is the clear conception of the whole at once.

—JOHANN KASPAR LAVATER

NOTES

Quick Hit Exercise for Gathering Information

1. Know your question.

2. Take your focus off the question.

3. Allow your focus to go deeply inward, into your body. We will call this your center.

4. Take a breath and expand that center outward until you reach your skin. What do your senses notice? What do you perceive, know, see, feel, hear, remember, taste, and smell? Where does your attention focus?

5. Take a breath and expand that center outward, beyond your skin, outward to all that you can perceive around you. What do your senses notice? What do you perceive, know, see, feel, hear, remember, taste, and smell? Where does your attention focus?

6. Take a breath and expand that center outward as far as it wishes to go. What do your senses notice? What do you perceive, know, see, feel, hear, remember, taste, and smell? Where does your attention focus?

7. Notice where your attention focused in each experience.

8. You have the information you need to formulate your answer.

Don't worry about whether you understand what the Quick Hit above was designed to do. It is enough for now that you experienced the exercise.

What You Experienced in the Quick Hit

What did you just do? You defined a target, a bull's-eye, a point that all of your information needs to hit. You then had to take your focus off the target—why? I'll explain. Look at anything within two feet of you and keep your eyes fixed on it. Within moments, you will notice there is distortion. You know what you are supposed to be looking at, but you can't really see it anymore. This is true of your target as well. Your information is actually in the periphery of your attention and is stored, as it is gathered, mostly by your subconscious. Once you have your target, it is stored in your memory, which takes less than a second. This frees your senses to extend their perceptions to other elements that have an effect on the target, that exist around it, within it, and that define it.

In short, to answer your question fully, you need to know more about your target and about everything around the target. Everything is a system, within a system, within a system. In this exercise I had you start "within" so that you could really start to identify the experience of following your attention to the different places it can lead you on your path to forming intuitive answers.

So, What Is Intuition?

I'll start by saying that nothing fulfills me more than being able to teach people how to develop their natural sense of intuition. It uncovers a set of powerful skills that they never considered possessing. To be in a room where a hundred people are uncovering these skills is my idea of an exquisite moment. So . . . what exactly is intuition?

Intuition is accurate insight and information that you have not gained through the everyday use of your five senses, intellect, or experience. It is a higher octave of your five senses. In short, it is information that you didn't realize was available, information that can guide you toward your truest, best possible self. The key to a successful life is a smooth path, a quick transition when you hit a bump, and the ability to instantly make the next move correctly.

Children, ideally, have their lives guided and smoothed by the adults around them so that their perceptions and intuition are contained and directed into compassion, creativity, and community. Smooth paths are rare for adults, who interface with a huge and ever-changing world and have to confront new situations in quick succession, often without any downtime. In the absence of a smooth path, a solid intuitive reach is essential.

What do I mean by intuitive reach? Intuition gives us the

ability to communicate with our world at a distance, to perceive the future, to see the outcome of taking different paths, to find in ourselves fully mature resources, skills, and responses that are accessible only through our ability to tap into the infinite field of information and communication that intuition provides. Intuition is a powerful tool in guiding yourself and others in every capacity of life, from love to career to investments. Your own intuition can make accurate predictions, which in turn create successful lives.

YOU CAN USE INFORMATION GATHERING IN COUNTLESS WAYS:

- Extend all of your perceptions in space

- Review the past with perspective

- Research ideas in a comprehensive way

- Perceive the world around you in a less subjective way

- Sort correct data from incorrect data

- Illuminate areas of repression and dysfunction

. . . and many more.

I know, the question begs: how does intuition actually work? I have already explained that intuition is innate; however, I maintain that like all skills, it can be consciously developed. So where can we start? Intuition begins with a question. An intuitive reading is about asking yourself very specific questions. This is essentially the starting point—and precisely what I meant earlier regarding our ability to direct our energy and attention. By asking yourself the first question, you create a foundation from where your intuition can continue to inquire and respond to its own questions. After a while you won't even "hear" the questions anymore, and you will realize that you simply know the answers.

Of course, intuition is only as good as the questions posed to it. So, if you don't know your question, it is going to be hard to recognize the answer. For the purpose of the exercises, of life, and of the overall pursuit of happiness—even if you do not exactly know what your endgame is—it is your duty to yourself to explore it. Start here: what do you want to achieve, find out, experience, and improve? The more you can narrow each effort down to one goal at a time, the less confusion and scattering of purpose you will have.

Once you've asked your question, notice what information you receive, and by notice, I mean *simply observe*. The information may come in various forms, or it might not come at all. My beginning students often say, "I'm not getting anything" or "I'm blocked." Well, I am here to tell you that "blocked" *is* information. I tell my students to describe the block: who is it, what is it, when is it, how do you get around it, under it, through it . . . More often than not, those questions inevitably build the answer.

Everything you perceive in *any* way, including distractions, thoughts, and even intestinal gas, should demonstrate to you that something is always happening, bubbling there beneath the surface (no pun intended).

Over and over again, you will likely come face-to-face with your own resistance to the information you receive. You will judge the information, question it, and ask yourself what it could possibly mean. But when you begin to observe and document the information without judgment or opinion, and instead receive it with total equanimity, you will see that the significance of this intuitive data (and the significance of all of your perceptions, decisions, and actions) will lead you to be better able to manage your life.

As you begin to use intuition as a fact-finding mission, start by knowing what you *do* expect the answer to be, and then try to distract yourself away from what you think you know. You have to be willing to let in perceptions that you don't agree with, data that doesn't make sense in the moment, and distractions that you cannot apply immediately. Suspend your judgment long enough to find facts you did not even realize were there. After all, how long were we sure the earth was flat? When you are afraid to be wrong, you cannot freely use your intuition. Any judgment you pass on your intuited data is actually counterintuitive. The desire to be "right" eclipses your real targets and goals, which should be to report/document the information without feeling the need to qualify it. Your only job is to observe and then to document everything, whether you record it, write it, or carve it in clay tablets. Just get it down.

Instead of resisting the type of data that comes up, try to understand that our intuition has its own language, and it is important to learn how to perceive it. People tend to prefer one sense over another, but all of us always employ them all—whether we know it or not. People, for instance, who tell me that they don't "see" anything intuitively nonetheless give detailed visual descriptions once they allow themselves to use different language: "It feels yellow and large." Your intuition may speak to you in symbols or metaphors that make sense only to you. Symbols are representations of a dynamic or an idea. Your intuition, guided by your subconscious, will often use symbols to give you information when something about the information is too intimate, too foreign, too emotion provoking, or just too unsettling to emerge abruptly. Often your intuition will pick a symbol from your past; for example, that certain chocolate pudding you loved as a child might represent something totally safe and pleasurable. For this reason it is important to be aware of your symbols and familiarize yourself with their meanings. If your intuition and subconscious are using a particular symbol, it means that the symbol has had past significance to you. Learning the representational language of your subconscious is helpful, as symbols exist not only within us, but also throughout our environment. As you begin to know what your symbols mean, they are rendered useless, and your subconscious stops using them. In turn, you will begin to receive the information more directly.

Symbology is a language of its own, one where every single detail is rich with history and meaning. Practicing awareness of this truth will help you learn your own language of symbols and to work with the language of symbology in others, which is always unique and relative to the individual, culture, and era.

For many of the same reasons we rely on symbols, metaphors

are also important tools, and oftentimes they are employed by your subconscious to express ideas, dynamics, and qualities that are more comfortably expressed dressed up as something else. I always think of a metaphor as a story that really tells another story. I cannot tell you how many people in workshops have described a wedding as a business merger or vice versa.

Storytelling, in the conventional sense, is a way that we put incidents in context and give them an organized flow. When we experience memories, for example, which are stories of our pasts, we are receiving a complete picture to represent something that is actually going on in the present. It is the senses' way of using detailed, historical information to alert us to a current similar situation intuitively. The direction your attention takes in the memory is guided by intuition. One memory, for example, can trigger ten different stories depending on where your intuition goes—and this is precisely how intuition uses storytelling as an information-finding sense.

When we speak about intuition, we add another set of senses to our standard five. Intuition enables you to gain more accurate information so that you can make better decisions. Intuition may not show you the whole picture, but if it is working right, it will draw your attention to what you need to know for your question or goal. It alerts you when an area in your life needs attention and gives you tools to address the given situation successfully. Feeling, experience, instinct, and creativity all go together. Intuition is actually on the other end of the spectrum—because intuition is data that already exists; you are not actually creating anything. Intuition allows you to perceive a situation with detachment. You will find your own way to step away from conventional "knowing" and allow yourself the fresh impact of intuitive information.

Perceiving intuitive information is only one aspect of the exercise. You also want to seek out information that is *actionable*—which means information that you can act upon. For example, knowing intuitively that your heart will be broken in a relationship when there is nothing you can do about it is not useful and may even be harmful. However, knowing what to do now to be a stronger, more independent person is what you need to prepare yourself, and it is also something that you can tangibly do something about.

In the exercises throughout this book you will practice asking your intuition the right questions and begin to recognize which part of you is answering: intuition, intellect, emotion, belief, wishful thinking, or fear. This process will start to guide you away from harmful and confusing patterns and direct your intuition to information that is *useful, accurate,* and *actionable*—three very important words that I will use again and again. Here is why each word is vitally important.

Useful: If someone walked up to you and said the sky is falling and you didn't have time to move out of the way or prepare in any meaningful way for the event, the information would be useless. You get loads and loads of intuitive and other (intellectual, emotional, sensory, subconscious) information all of the time. Even if all of it were accurate, unless it is also helpful to you in some way and addresses your needs, it is nothing but noise. Because we are already accustomed and conditioned to so much noise, we tend to miss what is useful; it's like trying to find matching socks in a messy drawer. If you stay hung up on the useless information, your ability to function is compromised. With practice, however, you can train yourself to focus on useful information and create a place of peace where the noise used to live.

Accurate: Intuition gives you accurate data that addresses your question from a fresh perspective. Intuitive data, as with all other kinds of data, is not always interpreted correctly, and therefore there is margin for error. Often the mistake occurs when the intuitive thinks he is answering one question but is really answering another. Consider the scenario where a person wonders, Will this meeting go well? Let's say the person loses the deal in the course of said meeting but instead gets a great date out of the whole thing. The truth is that meeting did indeed go well, but had the person been more skilled in intuition he would have closed the deal as well, which was his original target/goal. This type of twisted fate simply means that we need to learn how to refine our targets. With thirty years of practice I still miss sometimes, because learning to use intuition is an ongoing process. The good news is that you have your entire lifetime to practice.

Actionable: In other words, can or should you do something about it? It is the rare case that you cannot change something that affects you by either changing the event, preparing for it, or avoiding it (working on the issues in your marriage before the trouble starts, selling your stocks before the market crashes, not taking the job at the company that is going to fail in a month). However, sometimes as information (intuitive and otherwise) is evaluated and delivered, the recipient is too ill informed or ill equipped to take action or, worse, is put into a state where she is actually disempowered by the information and less able than before to take action. My favorite example of this is when someone tells you to leave an abusive relationship and then goes on to list the reasons why you should. Had you been equipped and prepared to leave, you would have left, so this advice just makes you feel more powerless and takes your focus off what should be your actionable formula of gaining your autonomy, expanding your social group, and so on. Your own intuition, when listened to properly, should help you find a way of preparing yourself and making the right moves without scaring yourself into paralysis. Disempowerment is the nemesis of intuition because it allows the subconscious to protect you from the truths you need to be listening for. Alternatively, when you practice empowerment, your intuitive information will follow in abundance.

There are four other concepts that we'll be using throughout the book that also deserve some discussion: *target, attention, embodiment,* and *integrity.*

Target: When I ask you to define your target, I am essentially asking you to identify your question or objective. What will you use your intuition to find out more about? It may be a person, a company, the news, the market, or it can simply be the question "Is there anything I need to be aware of right now?" Your subconscious will fill in the blanks. In time you will start to understand that even the narrowest question is really broader than it seems. I'll give you an example: "Will I get the job I interviewed for today?" It would seem to be a simple yes/no answer, right? But your attention, regarding such a question, will naturally move in a million directions. Yes, you very well might get the job, but you may not hear about it immediately and in the interim find something else that you think you will enjoy even more, or you may realize that the person who interviewed you did not have your best interests in mind. Define your target as narrowly as possible when you can, and allow intuition to give you the broader, bigger-picture information as well.

Attention: In order to use intuition as a separate and unique tool, apart from our immediate sensory awareness of our environment or the wonderful storage facility of intellect and memory, you need to redefine attention. Right now, look at something in the room and keep your eyes on it. Every time you think of something else or experience something else bring your attention back to what you have chosen to focus on. Now, the next time you get distracted, whether it is by a thought or a noise or some other object, make *that* your new focus. Notice how many of your senses need to be reigned in to keep your attention on each object that you choose for more than a second (if that long). Attention is what creates your awareness. There are many things around you and inside of you, but your attention is where your perceptions are concentrated. We all have our attention on many places, people, thoughts, feelings, and sensations at one time. Much of what we are aware of we do not even identify. Intuition uses your attention to identify what information is important to answer your questions. When I say, "Follow your attention," I am simply asking, "What do you notice right now?"

Embodiment: Embodiment is the full sensory experience of anything. It includes everything that the senses experience both internally as well as externally. Embodiment is when you experience something with all of your senses, as you should always aim to be doing—life in the moment. You feel, see, hear, taste, think, remember, speculate, and are fully present and aware and able to detail your awareness. This encompasses both your inner awareness and awareness of the outer world around you. Right now, you are not just experiencing yourself and your senses, but you are also using your senses to evaluate the room you are in, what is coming next, what has just happened, who is with you, what is going on around you, and what it requires of or means to you. You are doing this all of the time. Intuition asks you to use this same ability not only to be fully present with your senses and awareness, but to move it around in time and space, into another person or even a hypothetical situation.

When I ask you to embody "you," I am asking the following: experience your most powerful, healed, and joyful you. We will speak more about this in the chapter on healing, and we will work to perfect it as you also master your sense of telepathy, which involves sending a convincing embodiment to a person or situation.

Integrity: Intuition will not necessarily make you a better person. That is your choice altogether. As you hone your intuitive skills, you will find that—along with all the good it can do—intuition can also help you to manipulate people and situations, lie in a language the other person will believe, steal effectively, and so on. Your sense of integrity, however, will not allow you to do things that you truly believe are wrong. But if your integrity is loose, you have the potential to cause significant damage. Ultimately, the quality of your life is equal to the goodness and clarity of your actions and intentions. If you direct your focus into knocking things down to get ahead, you may find yourself living, well, in ruins. It is important also to learn more about what your integrity is, what you love, what you value, what you believe, and who you would like to be in the world so that you do not do things in a way that you will later regret, so that you create the life you want and not just pursue a single goal that undermines that quality of life.

As we discussed in the introduction, "intuition" is part and parcel of other distinct yet related abilities, such as telepathy, body heat, healing, remote viewing, precognition, and mediumship. I say "distinct," but in practice these skills actually overlap greatly. In fact, I have never seen a person use one intuitive skill without a bit of another one somehow mixed in. You will tend to favor one skill over another, but the idea is to understand them as separate aspects of your intuition, so that you can learn how to integrate them more usefully.

Let me remind you that intuition is not a new tool. It has been used since the beginning of time, even before we had actual language for communication or the written word to share what we know with one another. However, as I have noted, applying any of these intuitive skills in your own life is often challenging. This is because you are your own most challenging subject—in large part because you know and protect your issues instead of confronting them head-on. For this reason, the daily exercises are especially important, as they help to decondition your instinct of self-protection, so that you can access the intuitive information that you need to move forward. Again, when you use your intuition in your daily life, you will likely be using all of the skills in this book together. If you seek intuitive information on a particular question, you may start with your remote viewing to get the physical layout of the problem but quickly use mediumship to experience the issue from the inside out; simultaneously, you may call on telepathy to hear the many positions on the topic, while also using healing to introduce a catalyst for a better outcome.

Think of this process as some kind of conscious reassembly of yourself, a re-encounter with your deepest sense of self, and a process that is only rendered possible if your perceptions are open. Once they are unlocked, you will be able to sense other people, situations, aspects of the future, and diverse points of view in the past and even travel psychically outside of your immediate environment. Once you understand the potency of such intuitive openness, anything you think of will interrupt the conditioned privacy of you being alone inside yourself. You will see that every iota of information you receive is in some way tied into some bigger picture of reality and able to be perceived by everyone around you.

The key to achieving this level of clarity has a lot to do with *intention*. You need to consciously create sacred space, sacred time, and even a sense of ritual—all of which forge a new awareness.

What exactly are sacred space, sacred time, and ritual? Well, they are different things to different people. *Sacred space* could be a simple state of being you can replicate reliably, where your consciousness can be present to feel, or it may simply be a physical place where you will always be reminded of yourself and your connection to whatever nourishes you from the inside out. Some people have a particular space where they do their intuitive work, but I encourage you to remind yourself that every moment is worthy of sacred space. Your intuitive self needs to function in your moment-to-moment-on-the-train-at-the-office-getting-a-thousand-things-done-at-once-while-stirring-spaghetti-sauce-

and-brushing-your-teeth state of being. Your sacred space is where you go to connect with yourself. Sacred space, sacred time, and ritual are ways of affirming that the endgame is your peace of mind and total contentment with yourself and the life you live. My neighbor's sacred space is her morning visit to Mass. My father's sacred space occurs behind his desk in his office surrounded by his computer, phone, medical journals, mementos of gratitude from past patients, and a ready supply of almonds—unroasted and unsalted.

Sacred time, however, is actual time that you allot—be it a moment, an hour, one day a week, an increment of time however large or small—that you commit to yourself for the sole purpose of connecting to the deepest parts of yourself.

Rituals are those repetitive, comforting routines that help you connect to that depth within. For some it is knitting, for others it can be yoga, cooking, drawing, gardening—or any other number of activities that promote personal calm and wellness. Your sacred space, sacred time, and rituals probably already exist in some way. Your sacred space may be your bed or your favorite chair. Sacred time and ritual may be the few minutes after your workday when you glance at the sports page, or it may be that first cup of coffee you brew in the morning at home before the day begins to unfold. My standard is to take off my shoes, put on one of my own audiotapes, and sink in silence into my couch. In the absence of my couch or much time, I simply take a moment to experience my blessings (although almost always with my shoes off), to really feel, see, hear, taste, smell, and reflect on what is wonderful in my life in that exact moment. I also have little "altars" around my house where I put my projects and wishes, especially on my coffee table in front of my couch. The bottom line is that you need to be *intentional* about your time and sense of dedication to yourself. Some of you can listen to music or take five-minute naps. Everyone has some version of this comfort zone, which is exactly where you should have your antennae of intuition most acutely poised.

In a company, each employee should set up an "altar" (you may want to find another word for it, but see it as a place of focus, power, and comfort) in his workspace. Traditionally the group altar is the coffee room where people come together and affirm their direction, put forth their questions, and repower and reorganize their attention toward their work goal.

It is also helpful to make it a place where they are reminded that work helps them meet their individual goals. Things like color, seating (so that people talk), putting in a "good idea" board, and using the room for informal strategy get-togethers will help achieve this.

When you invite the business of so many broadened perceptions into your awareness, your sacred time, sacred space, and rituals need to become more conscious and effective, so it is important to remember that you can alternate between "sacred" (connected to your own inner awareness) and "engaged" (functioning in the world from moment to moment), almost without stopping to make the actual switch. But because your attention will be gathering so much useful, actionable information as you begin to work with your intuition consciously for the first time, you really need to ensure enough inner quiet time, lest you wind up feeling stressed and burnt out. When you learn to work with your intuition, when moments of crisis arise (which they inevitably do, as such is the human condition), in order to act correctly, you will be able to become hyperaware of what is going on, and you will also know when it is time to shut down and tap into the calm. This will all come with practice.

Treasure this process. It is the hidden gem of growth. We all believe that our life goals include creating the perfect business, finding the ideal lover, or some other peak experience that we believe will define our success, but the truth is that between the lines of all of those lofty aims and goals, what you should really be looking for is *you*. When you find you, the intuitive you, the powerful you, the loving you, you will always have a wise counsel, someone to show you the beauty in life, someone to talk to who will be consistently and unconditionally honest, reassuring, and accurate, someone who will reason with you when you need it and always act only in your best interest. You will have yourself fully, and you will never be alone.

Information-Gathering Daily Process

During the day, when your mind wanders, try to notice where it goes. Unless these thoughts are ones you typically tend to over-think (concerning health, abandonment, or whatever your issues may be), allow yourself to generate questions about this area of your life. It is also very important to know the difference between intuition and circular thinking. Consider that if your thoughts were intuitions instead of patterned circular thinking, you would have resolved the habitual issue or problem ages ago. Intuition doesn't allow you to focus without resolution unless your subconscious goal is to keep yourself stuck, in which case intuition, when trained, will start to nudge the subconscious away from that goal.

Nothing new comes of thinking and rethinking in the same old way. Your weary, constant concerns will not direct you to their answers or any other ones. You have to take your "eye" off the mind's habitual dance to find the new directions that will solve the old concerns. If you cannot stop having those recurring thought patterns, take a deep, forceful breath and direct your focus to the flow of the breath. Forget the questions after you create them. Simply thinking of them is enough for your attention and intuition to begin their search for answers. Try to follow your mind's wanderings, and keep following them until they take you to some level of understanding.

Here's another suggestion: your intuition will be free to travel when you engage in a repetitive activity that does not require your complete focus. Activities such as washing dishes, walking on the treadmill or outside, swinging on a swing, or repeating prayers that you know by heart are all examples of things you can do to help your intuition flow. Try to limit activities like watching television, chatting on the computer, or playing video games, which are not conducive to the inner work we seek to master. Here are some ideas to consider as you begin consciously to follow your attention and generate the necessary questions:

- Where do I choose to direct my intuition today? What are my goals? What problems/issues and relationships am I trying to improve? Write all of these questions and answers down, so that your intuition has a concrete road map to work with.

- What are the issues I always think about that disturb me? Now say to yourself that you are going to distract your attention from these issues, knowing now that all this time you have been habitually confusing thinking with intuition. Begin training yourself now to focus more on your positive goals.

- Is there anything that I am so afraid of, anything that I feel so powerless about that my own awareness and intuition might actually hide the related details? Remind yourself that these potentially squelched details could ultimately help you to protect yourself and to create positive change.

- What might some of these areas be? What are the details that arise, and what are the details that I seem to want to avoid? Go there . . .

CHAPTER 3

Mediumship

Intuition is the supra-logic that cuts out all the routine processes of thought and leaps straight from the problem to the answer.

—ROBERT GRAVES

NOTES

Quick Hit Exercise for Mediumship

Intuitive skills cannot be fully understood until you have experienced them, but the irony is that you can actually experience them before you have any kind of understanding. So, before continuing, please take a few minutes, longer if you wish, to *do*—not simply read—this exercise. Don't worry whether you are doing the exercise correctly. We will discuss its meaning and relevance later.

1. Pick your target: a person, an object, or a situation.

2. Assume that you become your target by engaging in a private game of what I call "conscious role-playing."

3. Acknowledge that nothing in your current experience is about you any longer. You are your target.

4. Think in the "I," with your usual sense of "I" being your target.

5. Your body, your thoughts, your feelings, your needs, how you see and perceive the world, what you regret—everything you experience in any way, try to do so as your target. Allow yourself to follow your attention while being in your target.

6. Document your experience in full detail.

What You Experienced in the Quick Hit

If you thoroughly committed yourself to the exercise, you were probably surprised at how quickly you were able to "become" someone (or even something) else. Even if it felt like you were making it up or acting, chances are you got some amazing hits. Let's say that you feel the exercise didn't work for you (something that I rarely see with new students); even the mere attempt of taking on the experience and perspective of being someone or something else will access new areas of your perceptions and sense of judgment that you seldom use. Keep the information that you received from this exercise; you will start to see its relevance as events continue to unfold. Alternatively, if you were able to do this exercise with ease the first time, see it as a sign that you need to work harder on boundaries for reasons that will be explained later in the chapter.

What Is Mediumship?

Mediumship is the first intuitive skill that we employ as babies, which is why it makes sense to begin our development of intuitive skills here. Mediumship is the ability to merge so completely with something or someone else that we experience ourself as the other. We know that babies do not have a detailed sense of themselves as separate from the environment, so in turn, their state of mediumship is both elemental and instinctive. When you consider the above truth, mediumship—or the state of being the same as or as one with another—becomes so fundamental and quintessentially primal that experienced correctly, it returns you to a natural state that has always been underlying you.

Mediumship is also the esoteric skill that psychics tend to employ for what I call the "bump-in-the-night" skills like communicating with the dead, experiencing past lives, and speaking as "spirit guides." As such, mediumship is likely the least understood branch of intuition. We have all seen television shows or movies where a medium speaks to the dearly departed. Think Whoopi Goldberg in the film *Ghost*. Sometimes the medium even undergoes physical changes and looks like someone else, speaking in her voice, knowing her past, and even using her gestures. You can certainly employ mediumship to do this, and if you are doing a research paper on Cleopatra you might want to give it a try. Personally, I have enough living people in my world who require my awareness and attention to keep me from poking around in the world of the departed.

I know it is hard to wrap your head around this one, but mediumship is the ability to *become* the object of inquiry. Instead of viewing a new company, a market, a relationship, a political situation (as with telepathy, which we will explore later), you actually embody it. You might lose (your own) perspective in doing this, but you gain access to minute pieces of information that you would never have considered, allowing you a true sense of how the object views itself, what it is planning, what it needs, and what it hides. You can evaluate a relationship by *being* the relationship as a whole and asking yourself relevant questions within it, and you can feel within you parts of a company or business organization and how said parts work together to form a whole, as the whole.

YOU CAN USE MEDIUMSHIP IN COUNTLESS WAYS:

- To know a competitor's plan from her point of view

- To know how to sell your product from the market's point of view

- To know how people want to see themselves and be able to act on the information in a credible way

- To create change for people (and groups of people, such as companies or organizations) from the inside out

- To be able to experience the dynamic of complex situations in an integrated way

- To evaluate a company, market, government, or stock

- To know what another person is actually doing and how he defends his actions to himself

- To know what language a person or market will respond to

- To change yourself in the past

- To experience a loved one at a distance

- To understand a future situation

- To experience who you are becoming

- To experience and heal aspects of the person you have always been that might negatively impact who you are today

- To use your ability to be a medium to help someone else have a conversation with a person not present (and allow her to help you do the same)

- To evaluate what a friend, partner, family member, coworker, or even a company wants or needs

- To effectively masquerade to get a job done, close a deal, or appeal to someone

- To acquire a skill that you do not possess

. . . and so many more applications unique to your particular situation and needs.

As with all other intuitive skills, mediumship is one of those things that you engage in all of the time, whether you know it or not. It's as simple as that ever-common phrase we use over and over again in our lives: "Put yourself in the other person's shoes." You will find that you are becoming other people all of the time, worrying about how they might react, how they feel, what action they might take, what their opinion might be. A more evolved and conscious sense of mediumship emerges only after you have practiced being *you*. Only once you have grasped that will you have both a clear sense of self and a clear ability to become someone else. Imagine, for example, that while speaking to your employer you get a sense (through mediumship) that he is excited and ready to move forward but encounters some obstacles in presenting the changes to shareholders. While you may worry about the risk of letting your employer know that you feel this in your gut, the risk you take now, which is based on conscious assessment and intuitive truth, may very well make you the next company superstar.

Please Suspend Judgment

I am not going to try to make this chapter any less weird than it is. I can only encourage you to go with it and see and experience what you are able to do with this new information, to possibly unearth the beautiful mystery and power of being you. Mediumship is the easiest but also the least discerning intuitive skill. There is no need to evaluate, understand, or piece together information. *You simply are the information.* This is why it is so important to document your information in some way. Keep a tape recorder or pen and paper at the ready every day. If you are writing, you will want to document each exercise after you have experienced it—not during the exercise, when I want you to have the fullest, most present, and most authentic experience possible. If you are recording, you can report your experience aloud as you have it.

There is another excellent intuitive exercise called automatic writing, where the medium chooses the target, becomes the target as the medium, and then writes without stopping. Try it. You will often have little or no awareness of what you are writing as you write it, but, as you will see, it will directly address your target. Everyone is different, so whether you are a writer or a recorder, choose one, and stick with it. Document, document, document.

Leap into the Deep:
Mediumship Aerobics

If you can, I encourage you to do the rest of this chapter in one sitting. The idea behind what will follow is to help you experience in more detail and depth your natural ability to become anything or anyone. In order to do this it has to be aerobic. What I mean by this is that the experience of mediumship has to override your ego barriers long enough for you to have a genuine experience. You have to put in some elbow grease, be willing to sweat, and take a real leap of faith into allowing and assuming that what you are experiencing is what your target is experiencing. The aware-ness that you can do this, and the acceptance of this fact, does not just flow, because it feels threatening to let go of self that much. You have to work at it.

Everyone gets a sense of what mediumship is at different points of the exercise: some of you intellectual types may not have it at all in your waking life but later get a hit as you fall asleep, or in that twilight sleep that happens in the early hours, just before you awaken in the morning when the lines between your conscious and unconscious are soft and blurry. Take as long as you want with each aspect of the experience, but as I said be-fore, do not stop until you have done all of the exercises in one sitting.

A word about ego, which, contrary to popular belief, is a good thing. Ego is what allows you to experience and behave as a separate and conscious individual. This exercise will challenge those very healthy boundaries of the ego by putting it back in its rightful place—all by the mere task of embodying yourself.

Now, as odd as this may strike you, take a moment to simply *be yourself.* This is not as far-fetched an idea as it may sound. Even the simplest things such as hunger and feeling hot or cold can overwhelm you, distracting you from your essence. This exercise asks you to abandon the superficial, momentary iterations of you and tap instead into the totality of you—all of your thoughts and everything that is going on around you. Be aware now. If I em-bodied you, for example, if I *were* you, how would I feel? What would I notice and remark on? What would be the important things going on in your life that I would be aware of? What pieces of your past would I be stuck on? What would I be looking for?

What would I be grateful for? What questions would I be asking of myself? Jot down some notes of your observations.

Now let's turn it around: Be me. Really assume that you *are* me. You feel like me, you are where I am located right now. You are digesting what I just ate and thinking about what is on my mind. You know what I want to do and you know what I have just done. Every feeling you have is truly my feeling. You are me. Experience being me in complete detail. Allow yourself to be fully in the experience as if the person who was "you" a moment ago is in a corner looking down at you being me. Everything you experience right now you are experiencing as me.

You can do this quickly. Don't overfocus, don't search in desperation for the state I am asking you to find; simply assume that you are me by allowing yourself to be totally fluid, free of expectation, judgment, or a desire for a result.

Now be your country. You are not just thinking about your country or imagining your country—you actually *are* your country. What is going on with you? Where is your attention? What are you thinking, feeling, needing, and hiding? What are your plans?

Now choose someone you truly want to understand. Perhaps it is someone with whom you are having a difficult time. Become her. Experience this person in this moment. Notice where she is, what is going through her head, how she feels, how she feels about you, what she is needing now, exactly in this moment.

Now, go back to being you. Really embody *you*. The ability of becoming a medium is as elemental as the need to be able to return to becoming yourself.

Now, assuming that you gave the above tasks even the smallest attempt, how did you become me? Investigate your own process, the shifts in attention you made. How did you become your country? Did you allow your mental chatter and doubts to become part of the experience, to become the target's chatter, or did you begin to abridge the experience, edit and judge the information? Was it so easy to do that it was hard to come back to being you? What did you struggle with to fully become yourself again?

Once Again, Only This Time I'll Guide You

Let's do this in a more relaxed state so that you can allow the experience to happen. The following guided meditation will help you taste the state of mediumship. Remember, you can use mediumship to "be" anyone or anything. Let's give it a try now. Think of something or someone you need to understand—from that point of view. It may be a market you need to appeal to, or a view of your company in a way that you experience the complete dynamic to make effective changes. It may be a relationship, someone you love or need to negotiate with, hire, or influence. You may be at an impasse with a child, partner, parent, or employer. If you could become anything or anyone to understand the target more fully, what or whom would you become? Write the name of your target down.

Now, take a long, deep breath and let it out slowly. As you exhale allow your entire self to relax. On your exhalation release any tension from your body, and as you inhale again allow your internal space to expand and clear. On your exhalation, release any tension from your mind. You don't need to keep such close track of all of those thoughts, and on your inhalation allow space to be created in your mind and your perceptions. On your exhalation allow your feelings to flow out of you and allow the space that is usually occupied with feelings and emotions to become fluid and free. Don't worry if you are doing this completely or well enough. Allow all interference to flood to the periphery as you experience more and more space in your perceptions, in your body, and in your mind. Now, as you breathe, allow yourself to become your target in this moment, for example, someone you want to experience from the inside out, seeing the world from his vantage point, experiencing the day as he is experiencing it now.

Simply assume that you are that person. You are feeling what he feels, seeing what he sees, remembering what he remembers, looking toward the future with his expectations. You are this person. Don't wait for this to occur. Assume that it has already happened and that anything you are experiencing in any way is being experienced as the person you have chosen. There is no "this is really me"; you *are* your target. What are you thinking and feeling? Where are you and what do you want? What is making you uncomfortable and what is comforting you? Notice what it is like to be you. Follow your experience. Notice what you notice as the person you have become, as your target.

Take a moment to experience the target fully. Write/record as much about your target as you can. Now take a moment to embody yourself fully as you again. In fact, embody your best self to the degree that you can. Embody yourself as confident, happy, loved, and healthy. This is not always easy. A great deal of interference can come up when you endeavor to experience only the best parts, the strongest parts of yourself. Don't worry if it is difficult. It is worth the effort, and no one ever does it perfectly.

How was that experience for you? Did your attention go to different places than it would have if you were just being you? What surprised you? What didn't you know about your target that you know now? How would this change the way you interact with your target?

What you noticed about your target during the Quick Hit exercise may have surprised you. Perhaps you felt compelled to want to experience the target's Social Security number, what he was wearing, or even the color of his car. You probably noticed first if you were cold, hungry, comfortable, or sad, that your pants were too tight or your mind was on a concern about getting somewhere in time. If you stayed with the experience long enough, you probably experienced more and more detail. Some mediumship experiences occur so fast that noticing any single detail is almost impossible. Even if, at this point, you think you concocted the experience, if there is a detail somewhere in there, verify it. Verifying what you experience during mediumship will allow your subconscious to see this skill as useful and make it more available to you the next time you need it.

Now think of any structure that you would like to experience from the inside out. It could be the Great Pyramid in Egypt or a local business, anything at all.

On your exhalation release any tension from your body, and as you inhale allow your internal space to expand and clear. On your exhalation, release any tension from your mind, your thoughts—you don't need to keep such close track of all of those thoughts. On your inhalation allow space to be created in your mind and your perceptions. On your exhalation allow your feelings to flow out of you and allow the space that is usually occupied with feelings and emotions to become fluid and free. Now, as you breathe, become the structure you have chosen. Your thoughts, body, and perceptions are all from that structure's point of view. You *are* the structure.

What do you notice about yourself? Where are your strengths and weaknesses, what is your view on the world from your vantage point? What parts of you work well with your other parts? Which parts of you cause difficulty? How do you feel the world sees you? What would you like to change? Do you have any sense of how to change it? Now allow your attention, as the target, to go anywhere it wants to go and follow the experience. Experience the experience. You may find that different parts of your body are different parts of the structure, different places of conflict or achievement. Allow yourself to truly become the structure in an ever-deepening and detailed way. Take notes on your experience as you return to embodying your own best possible self.

Now you're on your own. Practice mediumship in a more alert state. Remember to document all of the information you receive. Pick something or someone that you really want to know about so that you engage your inner motivator, curiosity. You know the drill:

- Pick your target.

- Assume that you *are* your target.

- Nothing in your experience is about you any longer.

- Think in the "I," with "I" being your target.

- Report your experience, remembering that everything you experience, in any way, you are experiencing as your target.

Notice your surroundings, thoughts, feelings, memories, and interactions, which will likely come in bits and pieces and not always coherent ones. Be patient, be diligent.

Using Mediumship in Your Daily Life

As I have said, unlike with other forms of intuition, you don't have to wait for information with mediumship since you have *become* the information. By practicing this technique, *you* now are what you want to know about.

However, unlike precognition (which we will cover later), mediumship offers you no detached perspective. You are less likely to be evenhanded or even accurate about what is going on around the target because you have a point of view—you are the target.

The best use of mediumship is the quick "in and out." Using the Quick Hit at the beginning of the chapter, you can, in thirty seconds, know what you are looking for and become your target, with your attention automatically directed to the part of that target that addresses your goal. Get out by embodying your best self. Once you get used to doing this you will do it instinctively during the day (and night) when the situation calls for it. As with all intuitive skills, mediumship is best when it is a healthfully patterned, subconscious response to a call for a certain kind of information. What you now can only do with focus and control will, with practice, be a tool you benefit from without having to be aware of using it.

Another wonderful use of mediumship is to troubleshoot possibilities. Yes, I said possibilities. Let's say that you are a doctor and you have a few drug choices to treat muscle soreness. You don't know what the patient's chronic muscle soreness is from, but you want to resolve it in the least toxic and most helpful way. You might use mediumship to become your patient and experience how she would react to each drug, taking notes as always.

Let's say you are thinking of introducing a new product to your market in September. You can *become* your market and experience whether or not you will want this product enough to buy it. If the answer is no, you can switch the variables. Do you want it as a Christmas product or as a summer product? You can become a market that would want your product. What would make you buy it? Would the product have to change or just its marketing? You can try mediumship out in small, noncommittal ways that will have no ill effect.

As with all intuitive work, do not get stuck on noticing only what interests you (in the case of mediumship, the person, company, or situation you are trying to become). Notice, especially when you are doing mediumship in the future (more about this in precognition), what exactly is going on around you and how it affects you directly. As with other intuitive skills, it is important to notice what you think the target is like before you do the mediumship, specifically so that you are aware of your judgments and biases.

You will find that throughout the day you regularly have a sense of being momentarily flooded with being something or someone else. It may be an experience of being a world event, the person next to you, your partner—the possibilities are infinite. This is spontaneous undirected mediumship, and it is worth paying attention to. You would not be aware of it if there was not a good reason. It is trying to tell you something.

As you develop your other intuitive skills throughout this book, you'll discover that you can combine mediumship with them in various ways. For example, you can mix mediumship with precognition. You can be the dollar a year from now (be exact with the date) or an industry in a decade. You can be your artwork in five years. The information you gain allows you to make adjustments now and to position yourself successfully and change events before they happen (always the best way). Or you can also mix mediumship with your ability to change the way the past affects you. There are many formative memories you have where experiencing them from another person's point of view would be transformative for you. Healing (which we will also cover later) is a dynamic process, and mediumship can change a past event that has to this point crippled you in some significant way.

You can mix mediumship and self-healing. On my father's side of the family there is a lot of skin cancer. My father has surgery to remove these cancers a few times a year. A skin graft from his forehead now makes up his nose because skin cancer ate away so much of it. Thanks to a wonderful surgeon, he is still a very handsome man. I lived on a beach in Italy, in the sun from dawn to dusk, burning, peeling, and freckling alongside my dark-skinned friends. After a while my freckles would connect, offering me, the blue-eyed, white-skinned redhead, a bit of color.

Of course, with the wisdom of age, I was terrified that I, too, would get terrible skin cancer. I certainly fit the profile and had ignored my father's admonition to cover up and wear sunscreen. As I worked more on doing healing with others, I used some of the knowledge I gained on myself. Each day for a few moments I became the young me on the beach. I covered with sunscreen. I went indoors. Last week at my father's insistence, I went to his cancer specialist. He was surprised, given my family heritage, my coloring, and my history, that I had no evidence of skin cancer or precancers.

I have used a similar technique on my slight autoimmune disorder, which gives me muscle tenderness and a reddish facial mask. It only occurs when I am not resting enough or am under undue stress. Can you guess why it doesn't resolve? It is adaptive for me. I need it to tell me when to stop, rest, take time for myself. There is more on this in the chapter on healing, but for the purpose of learning self-healing mediumship, find a symptom now that happened because of a past behavior or trauma and use mediumship to go back to the younger you and change what you did.

Whether you are using mediumship by noticing its guidance as a daily practice, integrated into your routine, or directing it at a specific goal, this tool will give you the detailed and comprehensive information you need to rule the world from your couch. You will know exactly how to address people and situations using their own resources, language, and skills. The more you are aware of this ability, the less you will actually have to do to get your result. You will be surprised by how many new experiences, ways of experiencing, and points of view exist. All of this will round you out as a person if you allow it to.

Training Others in Mediumship

Training others to develop this powerful intuitive skill is immensely rewarding for both teacher and student, whether one-on-one or in large group settings. It is the easiest intuitive skill to teach, and students can get immediate feedback on their results.

Have each person in a group choose a target they want a medium to become.

In a group, pair people up and tell them that they are going to take turns having conversations with their partner as the target they have chosen.

Tell the person who has chosen to be the subject first to simply give the medium a name with as little identifying information as possible (for example, "Jackie," without saying who Jackie is or whether Jackie is a man or a woman). Instruct the medium to assume that she is that person, not to try to figure out who the person is.

Tell the subject that he has a few minutes to have a conversation with the medium. The subject should begin the conversation. Both parties should take notes and cross-reference afterward.

- Sometimes the target will be a man, but the medium will express herself as a woman or a company, or as your husband. This is not a reflection on the sexual orientation of your target or the medium being inaccurate. As a subject, stay engaged in the dialogue and allow for the possibility that accurate perceptions may be presented metaphorically or symbolically.

- Ask the medium to verbalize quickly without stopping much until the subject asks another question. This will keep the medium from slipping back into herself and allow her to give detailed information that would be difficult to give if she could "hear" herself expressing it.

- A medium may express herself in a manner that is embarrassing to her when the exercise is complete, although chances are that she won't even remember much of the experience. Simply remind her that she was someone else.

- A medium's senses often experience pieces of the target and then the details fill themselves in. Perhaps the medium is timid to be saying these things as a person, so she expresses herself as a company.

- People don't often experience their name, rank, and serial number. The medium is experiencing what the target is experiencing. How often do you sit around thinking or feeling "I am woman" or "I am in New York"?

- The medium will tend to express herself as the target would. If the target won't talk about love in person, for example, it will be hard to get to through a medium, but the medium does have the opportunity to change.

The feedback to give, especially in an ongoing group, is not how accurate the medium was in the moment but how productive the results of the negotiation were after the fact. By "negotiation," I refer to the dialogue that occurred with the medium outside of herself, as something/someone else.

The Dangers of Mediumship: Maintaining Your Boundaries

Once your mind gets over the idea that you can't become someone or something else, your mediumship skills will blossom quickly. As with telepathy, mediumship is something that directs your life all the time. You are always experiencing a whole universe of people inside of you and thinking that the experience is your own. (The difference with telepathy is that the communication is mostly in action and ideas, whereas with mediumship you experience the other person directly.)

The simple act of getting everyone out of you for a moment may give you the direction, clarity, and courage you need to do many things for yourself that you have felt prevented from doing in the past. A gift of mastering mediumship is the ability to recognize when you have full possession of your power and attention, and when someone else's needs, pain, and goals are being felt and acted on by you as if they were your own. Combining that with the embodiment of your best possible self—healthy, happy, fulfilled, and at home with yourself and your world—is the best way to grasp the power of mediumship. Not easy, but incredibly powerful.

In being able to identify what mediumship is and what is your projection, you need to practice being a medium so that you can also practice being you (embodying) without so many people inside of you. I tend to like the "one person per body" rule in daily life. The daily practice of embodiment will help you recognize when you are being a sloppy, overindulgent medium.

Surround yourself with people who have attributes that you want to acquire and allow yourself to learn as you teach, as you do in every interaction.

Developing Mediumship Even When You Sleep

Speaking of daily practice, you can even develop this skill at night, when other parts of your mind are accessible.

Before bed, write down or simply take a moment to be aware of the confusing interactions you have had during the day, as well as the ones that may have positive potential. If you worked through this chapter today, your targets will automatically be on this list. You may also want to make a list of who is inside of you, whose voice came out of your mouth today and got you in trouble, or who didn't allow you to speak your piece from within yourself. Who did you act like when you didn't act in your best interests today? Make a list of these people or dynamics and throw them out or perform some other ritual to reclaim your inner space.

In the morning, when you wake up, jot down where your attention goes. Memories you wake up with, ideas, feelings, new points of view, desires, anxieties. During the day refer to your list. You may find that your sleep state prepared you, through mediumship, to be able to better navigate others' desires and points of view and achieve your goals more easily. You may also find that your targets already seem to have shifted, as if they had experienced you in a way that created agreement. This is the active use of mediumship. You can change people from the inside out, something we will cover in more detail in the chapter on healing.

Developing Mediumship through Daily Practice

It helps to use a workbook to record your experiences (see page 22), because the feedback you receive might not be immediate, and you will want to track your process. Here are simple daily questions you can ask yourself, as a way to tap into the use of mediumship:

- Whose point of view would it be helpful for me to experience today? Quickly use mediumship to get a hit on these people.

- What situations do I need to know more about today? Use mediumship to get a hit on these situations.

- Be *you* twelve hours from now. Ask yourself, How am I? Using this information, what can you do right now to have a better, more successful, more productive day?

- Choose a situation from your past. "Be" someone other than yourself in the situation. Ask yourself, What did I learn from this experience? How does it change my perception of the past? How can this change help who I am now?

- What choices do I have to make about my life? Use mediumship to try on different choices and experience the results.

The more you practice mediumship, the more effective your skill will become. Be creative; the possible uses are limitless and present themselves daily. Here are some other examples:

- Notice when you are not feeling like yourself and allow yourself to be aware of who or what you are experiencing and why.

- When you need to employ a skill you are not proficient at (math, small talk, public speaking, negotiating), use mediumship to become someone who is. Who could you become right now who could give you the experience of being expert at negotiating (or whatever)?

- Mediumship is a wonderful tool in times of stress to give yourself a break from being you. Use mediumship to return to a calmer former you, or to someone else altogether who can relieve your stress.

CHAPTER 4

Telepathy

There are only two ways to live your life: One is as though nothing is a miracle. The other is as though everything is a miracle.

—ALBERT EINSTEIN

NOTES

Quick Hit Exercise for Telepathy

1. Choose your target.

2. Be clear about whom you want to send the message to.

3. Be clear about what you want him to do or feel when he receives the message.

4. Be aware of any strong emotions or hidden agendas that might interfere with your sending a clear message to this person.

5. Allow your intuition to make you aware of any reasons that this person may not want to respond to your message.

What You Experienced in the Quick Hit

In the Quick Hit, as with intuition and mediumship, you chose your target. A clear sense of your target is essential in telepathy, as people, situations, and markets change from moment to moment, so you want whatever message you send to "be" as it is now. You may have used a combination of senses that come most easily to you to represent your target: a little seeing, perhaps a little feeling, some knowing, maybe her scent, or the sound of her at an exact moment. In any case, it was probably a mix of perceptions.

You then chose your goal, which in this context was the message. The point here was to have a clear goal or message, or some way in which you want the target to respond. Once you chose that goal, you might have experienced other messages that might've been "tangled" in your desired message.

You then allowed intuition to find any resistance in the person to the message. If you send a message in a way that hits the target with resistance, you must remind yourself that there is usually another way in. Just as with any dialogue or argument, ideas need to be delivered by a route that is easy for the target to accept and digest.

Once you had an awareness of all of the above elements, you really did not have to do anything more to send the message. When you spend that much mental energy on refining something, you are sending it already. The gift and difficulty of telepathy is that you are sending telepathic messages all of the time, whether you choose to or not.

What Is Telepathy?

Telepathy is commonly thought of as the ability to read minds, although I see this as a limiting definition of the true potential of this powerful, innate tool. Telepathy is your innate ability to guide the thoughts and behaviors of others; it is also your own vulnerability, so that you can be manipulated by the telepathic wishes or directives (conscious and unconscious) of others. How many times, for instance, have you felt angry, frightened, or insecure, only to later find out that someone was upset with you? How many times have you acted against your best interests because of someone else's subliminal messages? This unnecessary sense of mystery can stop now, because with the tool of telepathy, you are going to learn to send out the kind of messages that bring desired responses from the world around you. In this chapter you will master telepathy to change your future by changing this moment, yourself, and all that is pertinent around you. As with everything in this book, the idea is for these tools to translate easily to use in the business world. I always start with the individual as the example, so simply change my words to accommodate your business needs. Whether you use telepathy for your professional and/or personal success, you will be able to experience the effective use of your own telepathic ability and learn how to train it toward positive goals.

Telepathy is a useful tool to have in your day-to-day life, both to send messages appropriately and to defend yourself from the influences that come toward you. When you master the use of telepathy, you gain the ability to attract opportunity, to prepare adequately for it, and to recognize and possess it when it arises. You will also find that you waste less energy on being misdirected and manipulated by others.

In this way, telepathy helps you to chart a smooth, power-ful, and productive path for yourself each day before you engage with the world and can also help to reveal new choices about how to respond to what is thrown your way. One of the greatest gifts of a real awareness of telepathy in your life is that you will have, perhaps for the first time, the experience of really being in full possession of your own free will, with pure knowledge of your true self. You will enjoy being with yourself, and you will find that you are your own best friend, helper, intuitive, healer, playmate, and soul mate. I have rarely met the person who does not fall in love with herself when she is able to know and con-nect with her own essence for the first time, without the many telepathic interferences that she might ordinarily tend to assume are just part of her.

In recent decades there has been an interest within the scientific community in researching whether telepathy, or com-munication from a distance, really exists. If you are interested, I invite you to google "telepathy" and "research/science/studies." In this chapter, however, my goal for you is to see how telepathy works for yourself and to master the use of telepathy to change your life. You will see that telepathy, once you are aware of it, proves itself.

YOU CAN USE TELEPATHY IN COUNTLESS WAYS:

• To send clear, effective directives to people around you and get desired responses from them

• To defend yourself against the confusing, disorienting, and manipulative messages that others send you, consciously or unconsciously, all of the time

• To direct your messages with power and effectiveness and rid yourself of subconscious, hidden agendas that muddy your results

• To lay a constructive groundwork before you go into the office

• To negotiate cooperation

• To know what your opponents are thinking and planning and be able to convince them otherwise in advance

• To reclaim yourself and your life from old messages that you still carry inside of you, sometimes for decades, that derail your goals

• To problem-solve from a distance

. . . all from your couch (do you love me, or what?).

Below you will find some simple telepathy exercises. Please let them remain simple. Don't try to be a perfectionist about them and stress yourself out; see them, instead, as simple routines that will allow you to begin employing telepathy throughout your day.

What Messages Are You Sending Right Now—for Better *and* Worse

Before we address how you can use telepathy effectively, we must address the impediments to your natural ability. Right now I want you to be aware of the conversations you have in your head and heart that have no real goal. These include conversations with people who have hurt you in the past; arguments that, even if resolved, have no positive outcome; desires for acknowledgment that really bring you no tangible gain; discussions with the world at large or with a God that is too esoteric to bear real results in your life; even conversations you have habitually with yourself that are disempowering. I encourage you to jot some of these things down. The mind is a messy place, and having these things on paper will help you remind yourself to redirect your energies to the positive, powerful uses of telepathy that you are going to learn today.

Now, pick one of the conversations that you carry habitually in your head and allow yourself to be very conscious of the details. What are you saying, what are you trying to get the other person to hear? If you had a goal for this conversation, what would it be? If it resolved in your favor, what would that resolution look like and how would it help you? If, from these perceptions, there is a productive action to take, weigh the upside versus downside. If the positives are greater, take action. If not, put your attention on alert that this is no longer a conversation you will allow yourself to have. How do you do this? By choosing instead to redirect your attention to the productive conversations that help you with your new goals. This "weeding" of where we place our telepathy will become an ongoing process.

Another obstacle to your telepathy for furthering your own clear and productive goals is a lack of awareness of whose telepathy you are receiving. Sometimes you are the one who is habitually fixated on certain dialogues or people, but oftentimes it is the other people who are communicating with you. Let us first engage your intellect, so that you can be aware of who may be having conversations with you that may not be in your best interest. Make a short list. It could be your employee, your sibling, your ex, your parents, a friend, anyone who comes to your mind. In fact, you may unwittingly be in dialogue with the person you stole the seat from on the train this morning. To have *real* control of your telepathic ability, *you* need to be the loudest voice, the strongest and clearest focus of your own energy and space.

Chew on this: in many ways, free will is an illusion. We are forever sending and receiving "orders" to and from those around us, as well as those at a distance, but the truth is that we typically perceive these "orders" as coming from within ourselves. The more conscious you can become of which voice you are responding to, the more you can take control of your life's direction and begin to choose what you really want. Much of the telepathy you send to the world around you is based on patterns you have developed in response to life experience, as opposed to what actually works *now*, here, in the present moment. Learning to send clear telepathy allows you to represent yourself to others in a way that is effective and appropriate to achieve your current goals. The only way to do this is to simultaneously address these telepathic dialogues—perhaps with people you haven't seen in decades—that still manage to direct your beliefs, behaviors, and actions.

Telepathy is one of the many ways that we communicate with our environment and with one another. However, unlike more obvious personal attributes, such as our appearance and what our personalities are like, telepathy is a powerful *subliminal* tool that we can have. We can communicate with others clearly, wordlessly, and even from a distance—and sometimes, for reasons that I will explain later, as we sleep. We can learn to send out powerful messages of attraction that are specific enough to draw to us the people, yet unmet, whom it is important that we meet. Telepathy also alerts us to the patterned disappointments that those unskilled in telepathy draw to themselves over and over again.

Misuses of Telepathy

When you perform telepathy on someone else, you are creating or strengthening a connection to that person. If you do this with someone you are trying to get over—an old love, perhaps—you will be as engaged and affected by the telepathic message as the person you are messaging, which can be very unhealthy for you. I am not saying that you should never use telepathy to state your position, be heard, or say something you wish you had said, but be careful not to overuse it. Instead, remember to embody your own initial goal, separate and apart from your target, so that you can detach and proceed once you have communicated telepathically.

For victims of abuse (be it physical, sexual, verbal, or emotional), although the desire for healing is totally understandable, it is rarely the person who harmed you who will be the one to heal you. Be careful of using telepathy in a way that may traumatize you all over again. Given the potency of telepathy, don't be surprised if your target (the past abuser) later reaches out to you to continue the dialogue that you had telepathically, and be prepared to handle this, should it occur.

Sometimes, even with the clearest telepathy, you cannot get someone to do as you wish, simply because each person has his own sense of determination. You can, however, enhance your chance for a result by stating and restating your best case. If you keep beating a dead dog, however, it is time to ask yourself why you are not turning your attention to a more worthy goal.

Being the Captain of Your Own Telepathic Vessel

Even though much of your life is ruled by your subconscious, you *can* take control of your life in a moment. Allow that moment to be right now.

Throughout your day, check who and what is recurring and reappearing in your mind; before going to bed is an excellent time to notice the issues, problems, hopes, pleasures, and people you are thinking about. Often these thoughts represent telepathic messages from others, in many cases messages that they themselves are unaware of sending and that you may want to consciously disengage from. Remember, the more you are the one in charge, the more of your own power you will have to direct toward change. As far as telepathy goes, I try to stick by one general rule: one person per body.

The notion of free will is challenged when you really experience telepathy and witness how many people's messages and goals sneak into what you think of as your own free will, especially in close relationships. I cannot stress the importance of really experiencing your own sense of self, at least for a few moments each day. It will clarify and simplify your life and allow you to build a life that suits you, with only conscious compromises.

The way to tap into this sense of self is through embodiment, an intuitive tool we covered previously, and it is really the only psychic self-defense that works. Embodiment is the act of fully inhabiting yourself. When you are full of you, all that is not you is pushed to consciousness and you can decide whether or not you wish to have it as part of your motivation. The wonder of intuitive tools is that telepathy is counterbalanced by embodiment, and vice versa. In the second part of this chapter we will learn daily practices that clarify, direct, and enhance your telepathy so that it becomes an empowering part of your every moment.

Now, let us begin to use telepathy to create real and lasting change.

First things first: you need to be especially aware of destructive emotional states you may be sending out. If your boss pisses you off, let off the steam elsewhere, so that you can find the right telepathic position to resolve the issue in a way that benefits you. You can use telepathy to upset, derail, or disturb someone, but is this really the best use of your time and energy? This is a coun-terproductive use of telepathy; your focus should be on creating positive goals in your life.

We all get stuck on the right and wrong sides of things, but powerful, effective people focus on the behavior that gets the right result.

Let's run through a typical day using telepathy to help you "reset" yourself and the world around you. First, let us restate what telepathy actually is: telepathy is your innate ability to guide the thoughts and behaviors of others, as well as your own vulner-ability to the influence of the telepathy of others. Telepathy can be used from a distance, or even on someone you have never met.

Let's say that you are looking for a loving partner to start a family with. Your target becomes that person, whoever he or she may be. You may get an image or sense of that person, or you may not. It may be a "field" of people who would fit that crite-ria or imagined description. You would use the same telepathic protocol that you learned in the first part of this chapter, but you would send it to all available partners. The same technique functions for finding a great employer, the perfect doctor, a good friend, or a more loving community. Your bonus work is to be able to experience your target more clearly, and if you do not have what you are telepathically attracting already, intuition will step in to make your target more and more lucid each time you do the exercise.

A word of caution: I do not suggest that you use this tech-nique on a love relationship where your partner has rejected you. Remember the warnings: you will only hook yourself into the situation more. What I do suggest is that you engage in telepathic communication with the kind of person you want to attract and with the connection you want to have. If your old flame realistically fits the bill, he will get the message (as it were) and respond. Remember that an important element of telepathy is the shifts it creates in you as you practice it, allowing you to really become the person who can get the "yes" from your target. In my mind, this is the most healing and useful part of the telepathic process.

Throughout this chapter we will continue to use telepathy to reset your ability to better control your environment and the way you function within it. In order to do this you will have to do more than just read. You actually will have to follow the many exercises that are included in this chapter. In doing so you will dramatically change yourself and the responses that you receive from the world around you. Intuition—the ability to get accurate information from the energy that we all share, the energy that knows no difference between the past, present, and future—will help you experience the information and help to develop the ability that may have been lacking in your direct experience of living. Using telepathy is easier than using your imagination. You do not have to "make up" or "create" your telepathy. It will come to you. You simply need to follow your own thoughts and attention. I have been teaching this material for nearly thirty years, so speaking from experience and with great confidence I can say that I know you have this ability (whether you believe it or not).

The nice thing about telepathy is that you do not have to believe in this ability to use it. Many of you have already done it effectively by doing the Quick Hit at the beginning of this chapter. Think of telepathy as something working beneath your consciousness all of the time. Don't worry about whether or not you are doing it correctly or if it is your imagination at play versus real intuition. The effects of this chapter on your life will answer those questions for you. The beauty of intuition is that in following my directions, even imperfectly, you may come up with a perfect process for you that surpasses my own. Intuition is direct, accurate, and individual. You are your own best teacher. I am simply a guide to lead you toward this powerful part of yourself.

I strongly suggest that you keep a journal to make notes about the messages you send out, as well as the responses you receive. By documenting your own awesome ability to create positive outcomes for yourself using telepathy, you will live in the truth that *you* are a superpower. Also, when your subconscious and conscious self see in black-and-white that telepathy is a useful negotiating tool, and will protect you from losing your free will to others, you will free up the inner permission to use telepathy consistently and accurately in the future. It is an ongoing process of mastery.

Enjoy telepathy. Send me some healing messages and I will respond. You are now well prepared to chart your own course in the world using telepathy . . .

And well on your way to ruling the world from your couch.

How to Send a Telepathic Message

If you know how to send an email, let me be the first to tell you that you can also send a telepathic message. Let us now be more specific about how to focus telepathy in specific situations, starting with the basics. Here are a few important steps to prepare to send any kind of telepathic message.

- Pick your target. Is your target a group of people, a person, or a situation? Have a very clear sense of what/who your receiver or target is. Some of us don't "see" clearly. This should not hinder you in any way. You have many senses that can give you a clear sense of your target. You may feel her, smell her, or simply get a sense that she is there.

- Have a clear sense of what kind of action or response you want from your target. What do you want him to feel, do, express, and change, and how do you want him to perceive you?

- Notice any hidden agendas you may have in choosing this message. Do you want your boss to give you a raise, or do you want him to acknowledge your true value? Pick one and be clear and keep that other sneaky agenda out of your telepathy. Focus on the productive goal. Do you want your husband to feel bad about his behavior, or do you want to negotiate changes? Once again, be clear about your agenda and put your energy into your goal.

- Be aware of the reasons (that you know of) why this person may not want to respond to your message. Intuition or flashes of insight may give you some new reasons that you had not thought of. This is where taking some notes can be useful, so that when you are sending you can shift the way you send your message to a framework that the person might better respond to.

• Telepathy is not always instantaneous and doesn't always occur in real time. (It tends to work more quickly with someone with whom you already have intimate and regular contact, as you are in each other's feelings, thoughts, and experiences all the time anyway.) This is why it is essential to keep a log of the intentional telepathic messages that you send out, as the response may happen a week or two later.

Let's summarize our basic protocol for sending a telepathic message:

• Pick your target.

• Know your goal or the response you want from your target.

• Be aware of your hidden agendas.

• Allow an awareness of why your target may not want to respond.

• Be your message, with all of your senses (think "mediumship").

• Place your target in front of you.

• Be with your target by embodying and experiencing the connection between you.

• Be open to new information from your target and shift your message or embodiment accordingly.

You can do this for a few seconds or for a few minutes. It is helpful to repeat the telepathy on the target so that it becomes a repetitive part of their experience. Advertisers have proved that it is precisely the repetitive exposure that sells.

There are some points about these steps that we should discuss. It is important that you have a clear focus on the person or target in *present time*. Especially when you are trying to communicate with someone you have history with, you may find yourself "talking" to that person as they once were. Telepathy works best when intuition can give you information about who the person is *right now* and what they need to feel from you to get the response you desire.

It is also important to have a goal for the message. The goal might simply be to comfort or reassure the person, but without a goal the message is just like static and may not be clearly received.

One of the hardest parts of executing telepathy is to know what you really want to achieve. As we asked previously, do you want your boss to appreciate you or do you want a raise? These goals may actually be in conflict with each other, so stay clear about what you are feeling and wanting under the surface and be on guard not to muddy the signal.

Intuition about your target will automatically be engaged when you focus. You will be receiving a good deal of information about what the other person needs to feel, hear, see, know, and so on for you to get a "yes." I really suggest that you jot down this information as you prepare to practice telepathy and that you continue to be aware of new incoming information about your target.

Here is one student's example:

- Target: An employer he has met once.

- Goal: He wants this person to offer him a job.

- Hidden agenda: He wants to be included with the "big boys" and acknowledged for his special talents. He wants to make a lot of money.

- Reasons the target may not want to respond: The target has so many people who are more qualified to fill this job, and his focus is not on this person; the target will be a little wary of this person on first meeting him (in experiencing the person's wariness, the sender is alerted that he needs to seem direct and down to earth, and a good advocate for the target within the company); finally, a sense that the sender could help the target personally in his own life.

Now the sender needs to find the person in himself who can convey messages to the target. To do this effectively, part of the work is to actually *believe* the message you are sending. You need to do some internal work to embody the authenticity of your intention.

Be clear about whom you are sending the message to, and use all of your senses to get a visceral sense of the person in the present moment and experience him in front of you. Each of you will have one dominant sense. Some of you will be able to see the person in front of you, some will feel the person, and there are those of you who will just know the person is there. We all use a combination of all of our senses, but we are usually most aware of our strongest one.

When people send telepathic messages, they tend to send words. There are so many words already in our heads that this is a very ineffective way to send telepathy. You need to send a full-body scene, using all of your senses to engage all of your target's senses. You need to be in your own message.

Once you integrate all of these techniques into your life, they should only take a few seconds to perform. Don't get caught up in form or perfection. Your own intuition will help you do this correctly for your unique set of skills and needs.

A Word on Authenticity

Clearly, if you think your boss is a jerk, your colleague is a cheat, or your spouse is a wretch, it will be difficult, and often unwise, to change your true opinion of them on a dime. However, you can send an authentic message of acceptance, love, cooperation, or whatever else you need a person to experience by using memory (a scene from that one time she came through for you, made you laugh, or created something wonderful with you), or you can maneuver through your thought process until you come up with a few qualities or scenarios that are positive about the person (not always easy) and embody those. Since much of what we send is transmitted through the subconscious, the more conscious a positive "collage" you have of what you want to send, the more likely it will be to transmit more clearly.

You have to find something believable for yourself in the message you are sending before you can send it effectively.

Bedtime Telepathy

Sleep time is one of the most opportune periods to send telepathic messages, as the intended recipient is likely to be more open to receiving them. In sleep, both the sender and the intended recipient are less engaged in busy waking life's demands and structures and therefore are more receptive to the message and open to change.

We know that we are subconsciously sending out telepathy all of the time, and we also know that others are sending it to us as well. So it is important that we consciously make ethical and productive choices about what we will send and receive, especially during the powerful and vulnerable time of sleep. Let us prepare. Ask yourself:

- With whom do I want to communicate during my sleep? What is the goal for this communication?

- What situations in my life do I want to negotiate during my sleep? What outcome would I like to create from these negotiations?

- What issues or concerns within myself would I like to resolve during my sleep?

Sweet dreams, and I wish you productive negotiations and healing during the night.

Telepathy Processes

Telepathy is the intuitive energy that has the strongest and most persistent effect on your day-to-day thought processes and on how powerfully you are able to direct your energy toward your own goals without too many other voices getting in the mix. Practice is useful because it will keep you clear and in possession of your own volition.

In this process:

- You will send clear, effective directives to people around you and get desired responses from them. It is important that you do some of these exercises at least once a week.

- You will defend yourself against the confusing, disorienting, and manipulative messages that others send you, consciously or unconsciously, all of the time.

- You will direct your messages with power and effectiveness and rid yourself of subconscious, hidden agendas that muddy your results.

- You will repossess yourself and your life from old messages that you still carry inside, sometimes for decades, which ultimately derail your goals.

- You will negotiate and problem-solve from a distance.

- You will draw the right people and experiences toward you.

Telepathy Process 1

Here goes: just flow with your answers, and the rest will reveal itself. The conversation should flow into itself.

I need to end the conversation with _____

_____

I get the sense that _____
is talking to me. This is what they are saying:_____

_____

_____

_____

This is the response they want: _____

_____

_____

_____

I choose/I do not choose to allow this conversation to continue. I can/cannot give them the response they desire. If I can, I send it now. If I cannot, I allow intuition to guide me to my appropriate response.

What feelings are you having that are disturbing you? If you follow the feeling with your awareness, is it your feeling, or is it something being generated toward you by someone else? If a telepathic message is knowingly or subconsciously being sent to you by another, whose thoughts or feelings might these be?

Telepathy Process 2

This next process allows you to track telepathy and its responses and check its accuracy. Pick one conscious telepathic message to send throughout the day to a situation or person with whom you would like to experience a change.

Target: _____
_____

This is the telepathy I sent and the information I received in return: _____
_____
_____
_____

Result: _____
_____
_____
_____

What are my concerns? _____
_____
_____
_____

With whom or what am I having difficulties? _____
_____
_____

What would I like the outcome to be with these people or situations? _____

_____

_____

_____

What are my hopes and wishes? _____

_____

_____

_____

Adjust how you send the message to what you sense the person will respond to.

Integrate yourself and the person experiencing your message (so that you are experiencing both of you at once).

Notice the exchange and continue it for as long as it feels productive.

Telepathy Process 3

Now say these phrases to yourself every night before you go to bed:

- I commit to resolving these issues now, so that I can be fully within my power and create the life that I want.

- I commit to making contact with the people, groups, and situations that will help me become the person I want to be and create the life I want to live.

CHAPTER 5

Body Heat Telepathy

It is the silence between the notes that makes the
music.

—ZEN PROPHET

Quick Hit Exercise for Body Heat Telepathy

1. Choose your target. Your target can be someone you know, you would like to know, or "the woman of your dreams" whom you haven't met yet.

2. Allow your senses to find your target's "hot zone"—his desire.

3. Notice the information your senses receive when directed into your target.

4. Find those senses, those qualities within yourself, your own "hot zone," perhaps using the aid of a memory.

5. Experience a connection in the energy or space between you and your target.

6. Now *be* your target's "hot zone." Reach your embodiment of his ideal experience being both *his* ideal and him (your target).

7. Notice new information that you receive while doing this exercise, and adjust your being accordingly.

8. Be ready and open for body heat.

You first chose your target and allowed intuition to get a sense of your target in time and space. You then used your telepathy to identify the pleasure needs of another.

If you did this exercise effectively, you used your intuition to find those qualities in a being that would address such needs and desires in yourself, even if it required piecing together fleeting moments of you from various memories. You embodied those qualities and experienced the connection between you and the other person in whatever way you were able. You may have really felt the connection, or seen it visually, or just known it was there. Using breath and attention and one or more of your senses, you connected the attractive part of yourself to the target.

As the target began to respond, you intuitively sensed the response and adjusted what you were sending to create more (or less) body heat attraction.

What Is Body Heat Telepathy?

Body heat telepathy, or the exchanging of a mutually attractive and compelling full-body, sensory, experiential message to another person, can be used in many ways and situations. I will give you techniques involving telepathy to use throughout your day in a way that heals you and also transforms the way you attract the people in your life—even those you'd like to bring into your life.

Believe it or not, sometimes the best place to find true love is on your couch. Before you go to the party, the dinner, or that walk on the street and attract the same-old, same-old your same old way, by using body heat telepathy, you can become the person who can fall in love with someone right for you. With this tool, you will begin to notice a new sense of openness as you take out the garbage (literally and metaphorically); as you get on a train to commute to work; and as you decide that today you are actually going to talk to the telemarketers who call. Love happens in so many ways . . . but only when you are ready.

YOU CAN USE BODY HEAT TELEPATHY IN COUNTLESS WAYS:

- To prepare for relationships before you get into them

- To attract appropriate partners

- To discover attractive parts of yourself

- To share pleasure as a way of living life

- To know what others need to see in you to respond

- To put yourself in a more strategic negotiating position

- To appeal to your market

. . . all from your couch.

Although this chapter uses the framework of dynamic physical and romantic attraction, everything in this chapter is useful in your business life as well. A market has to fall in love with your product. Body heat works with your colleagues, neighbors, clients, and family (and the list continues, as most relationships in your life need a visceral, dynamic energy to flourish). I use the word *love* a lot in this chapter, and love is what you want the world to respond to you with and to the things you create. So you may use this chapter to find, evolve, or even properly end a romantic relationship and also use it to create a demand—a love—for your service, product, or anything else you value.

What Causes Attraction?

Every time anyone walks into a party, potential loves are drawn to each other as if they were always meant to be together. Pulses race, attention heightens, and somehow connections are made. The next months are a total frenzy. Then it hits: you are undeniably meant to be together. You both only now know it and felt it from the moment that you met.

A year later you can't stand each other. You are bored, disappointed, and with any luck not married. What happened? Chances are that this alleged "true love" had fit some familiar pattern. Perhaps the person reminded you of a beloved person from your developmental years. Or, if you got really whammied, perhaps you were an ovulating woman, which would chemically increase your attractiveness and predispose you to mate. Or maybe, ladies, you were on birth control pills, which tend to skew your ability to find genetically suitable mates. Another whammy: perhaps you were genetically dissimilar enough to each other so that your chemistry didn't interfere with attraction. After all, studies show that genetic similarity can interfere with the perception of attractiveness, a feature of mating that is useful for not passing down certain genetically inherited traits.

Here is another scenario. You walk into a party and you see someone whom you find irresistible. You try every way you know possible to make contact, but he simply doesn't notice you, or if he does, he doesn't seem interested. Let's raise the stakes: you are genetically compatible; there are common elements with each of your developmental love history/patterns; and the woman happens to be ovulating. What happened? What went wrong? And why were you not noticed?

Unbeknownst to you, the message you were sending out was off-putting to your potential partner. It was not what you looked like, what you were wearing, or your opening line (if you got that far). It was the complex, subtle, subliminal message, the telepathic sensory self that you were broadcasting. When I do a workshop, one of the most astounding discoveries for my students is how loudly their thoughts, feelings, expectations, and fears are broadcast to the people around them.

In order to change this scene into one where you and your guy or gal in question fall in love and ride off into the sunset, it would have to look like this: Picture the same scene as the one described above. All the signals are go for you, and yet your prospective partner shows no interest. This time, however, first you use your intuition to sense what your potential partner would need to experience from you in order to become interested; then you experience and embody you and this person together in a dynamic partnership of energy. In this way, you also experience the connection between these "attractive parts" of you, which won't work if you lie to yourself and try to be something that you are not. You must be your authentic self, the part of your authentic self that would attract that person. All of a sudden, the person, who up until this point has been oblivious to you, begins to notice you. Bingo. Another victory for body heat telepathy.

Let us take it even further. What makes someone attractive? Why are some people easily lovable and others work so hard for so little? This book aims to answer that question and explore the tools to attract love—the right kind of love—into your arms. Loneliness is endemic in our culture. There are many reasons that this is true, too many for me to address in what I intend to be a short and useful strategy for change. It suffices to say that if you have purchased this book, you already have a strong sense of how fundamentally love and connectedness define our lives—or at least *should* define our lives. This chapter is meant to be used, beat by beat, day by day, in your moments of success and those inevitable moments where you find yourself stumbling. I think most people would agree that no pain stings worse than that of a broken heart. For many of us, our hearts are broken from the very moment of our birth as we take on as our own the suffering and failings of those around us.

I have met people who have never been loved, but I have yet to meet someone who has not loved. That is because love and a sense of attachment are hard-wired into our being from the day we are born. The second the umbilical cord is cut, we look to attach to someone completely. If you look at it this way, we are born into this world loving. You have (and have always had) a fully developed innate capacity to love. However, oftentimes we find ourselves reaching for adults who have been so damaged that they are no longer able to love. These adults, usually our parents, have experienced too much loss, abuse, fear, or judgment to be able to retain their innate ability to love in a complete and healthy way. Because as babies we love, and our love grows with our developing awareness of the other in our first few years of life (until intellect and ego develop and intervene), as adults we often seek out the same kinds of people we knew when we were young, people who were unable to really love us well from the start. This pattern, this "love loop," needs to be reset so that you can choose a relationship that will give you what your whole heart wants, needs, and deserves.

The real secret to attraction is an *authentic self-love*. As you travel on the path to attracting true love, you will actually be reclaiming your own heart as your very own—whole, strong, pulsating, and powerful, as it was born to be. I write this as the owner of a heart in a lifelong process of healing. I was born to a woman whose greatest wish was to die. Many of you have similar stories. Unwanted, unprepared for, or simply injured unintentionally, you have been looking for your whole heart ever since your original injuries. Now you can look *with* your whole heart. What your whole heart looks for, it will find. The places deep in you, in your senses, memories, thoughts, and feelings, where you go to feel genuinely good—these are the places where you hold your power of attraction and not, as people often think, in the places that seem attractive and sexy. Think of the difference between an embrace where the person tightens their muscles so you can feel how in shape they are and an embrace where the person takes a deep breath and really holds you, or moves his cheek lightly across yours to feel your skin. Which do you think is more attractive and compelling?

The same thing happens in our own internal image of what we are attracted to. We either desire through our true needs and pleasures or through our damaged selves (and sometimes through a bit of both). The perfect example is the overweight person who is attracted only to thin people, or perhaps the shy person drawn only to bullies. However, this is not genuine attraction. It is neurotic compensation for work that needs to be done on the self. For example, an uncomfortable "perfect person," or one who is trying to appear that way, is likely to attract someone looking for the same self-imposed illusion. We want true love, but what we fail to see and understand is that true love is real, gutsy, and messy in the most delicious way—tactile, truthful, and passionate. True love is not blind, and it is certainly not based on a one-dimensional cardboard image of who your partner or you "should be." It is a process of discovery and mutual creation. True love is manifest as you honor and treasure the reality of a partner who honors and treasures you. Real attraction holds infinite possibilities for growth and change.

In a true partnership of love, one plus one equals an infinite number of possibilities for beauty, power, growth, and passion for each partner. Remember that you, and everyone around you, are always changing. You cannot negotiate lasting, loving change in yourself or a partner from a space of weakness. Only by experiencing your strength and your ability to take responsibility for your weaknesses can your most desirable partner be drawn to you. That doesn't mean that you have to be this totally balanced, perfectly healed, fully evolved person to attract your best life partner—if that were true, believe you me, we would all be alone. You need only be committed to the very essential, self-valuing *process* of healing.

Of course, just because you are attracted to someone doesn't mean that she or he is the right person for you to be with. I always tell my students that intuition can as easily help you find the next disastrous relationship as the next appropriate one. Intuition simply points you in the direction your subconscious wants to go, but in order to use this technique to bring true, supportive, passionate, healthy love into your life, you will need to do a bit of work on *whom* you are looking for and why. In fact, you may need to start with the question of whether you really want love at all. That may seem a ridiculous concept. Doesn't everyone want love? Well, at their deepest core, of course they do—but it is not always so black-and-white. You, for instance, may feel very lonely and think that you want a partner; however, your childhood experience of love may have been unsafe and unreliable so that today, you subconsciously sabotage yourself. Some of you may not even have the wherewithal to make contact, which is actually a self-defense mechanism to protect yourself from further injury. Some of you may be stuck in relationships that are not working or trying to hold on to a person whose attention you are losing or already lost. By repatterning your "love code"—whom you choose, why you choose, how you allow yourself to be treated—you can safely allow yourself to let love in, to leave when it is time to go, and to reignite the heat when love dies down.

This applies in other areas of your life as well. Who, what, how, and why you end up in a certain position in your business/success/connections can also be addressed in this manner.

Once you master how to use body heat telepathy in your romantic relationships, you will find that the improvement extends to all of your relationships, including your professional ones. Close relationships, long relationships, and intense relationships: deep, enmeshed connections in all of their forms are the most difficult targets to define and experience clearly. There is so much history, hope, fantasy, and projection in these relationships that they require the greatest internal adjustment for you to handle them in a new, powerful, and productive manner. Once you master this skill, you will have your highest telepathy credentials.

Who Are You Searching For?

Right now, ask yourself: What in your history is keeping love away from you? What might you be protecting yourself from? Unlike the powers of intellect or imagination, with intuition we simply wait for information. Anything that comes to your senses, thoughts, feelings, memories, or even what you notice in the room is information from your intuition to help you solve the riddle. Information can come from seemingly odd places, such as a friend you haven't thought about in years who pops into your head, or an old song that comes to mind, or any kind of distant memory. Let your intuitive attention fill in the blanks of what it is trying to direct you toward or have you experience. Remember, with intuition and body heat we *wait* for more meaning instead of *looking* for it. What happened with the friend? What are the words to the song? If you are using this book for business, the same process can apply to you, your company, and anyone who works for you. General intuitive information gathering, joined with telepathy, will guide you securely to what/who you want and the parts of you that need strengthening to have it.

Your wounds can become your strengths. Wherever you are injured, if you exert the courage and work to heal, that place will become your unique gift in love and in all interpersonal relationships. This part of you develops into a mature, sensual, treasured aspect of the way you love. It is a gift that you give yourself, not one that your parents, or anyone else for that matter, gave you. You can send this part of you outward telepathically with great power because you have spent time and attention knowing and understanding its intricacies. The gift of healing is that every injury, once healed, produces a powerful strength. You need to know your self—your true, pure self—to some degree in order to find your true partner. Body heat telepathy will work on most people whom you want to attract, but to attract the person with whom you will share a really joyful and lasting relationship, you need to investigate some of the qualities you may think you need in a partner and discover what your whole heart—the one that has not been judged and damaged or influenced to your detriment by the expectations of others—truly wants.

You may want to take a moment to allow intuition to help you consider whom your parents would have wanted (or not wanted) for you. Sometimes this helps us home in to an ideal that we did not even know we entertained. More than just looking at the qualities of the person, run through a day in your life with this person. What are you both doing? How do you feel about each other? What do you enjoy most about this other person? What does he or she know, love, and understand about you that allows you to feel at home?

Often our shopping list for a partner includes things that we feel we are not. For example, if you don't feel that you can have a significant impact in the world, you may seek a partner who is naturally successful. If you don't feel attractive enough, you may seek a good-looking partner who validates your lack of physical confidence with his or her own good looks. Our shopping list may include a desire to compensate for childhood privations or injuries. I, for example, was not taken care of as a child, and an early romantic choice was someone who I thought would take care of me; of course, there is always a high price to pay for compensative loving. It is time now to investigate where in your love ideal is a compensation for what you feel you are not, which keeps you from looking for someone whom you can really feel deeply connected to. Intuition gives you information about this search in an immediate, accessible way.

You don't have to struggle over these brief questions; simply notice the sensory and thought impressions that come up for you and take a moment to experience them. If it feels heady and ponderous, then it is not intuition. We are so well taught to over-think everything, but this is not how intuition functions best. Intuitions give you a trail to follow. You can and will, automatically, think it through later.

What Body Heat Messages Are You Sending out Subconsciously?

Let us begin with the idea of full-body experience. Most of us do not experience our senses fully, or even come close. What are you tasting *right now*? Feeling? Smelling? Seeing? Hearing? Thinking or remembering? Most of us live outside of our own sensations. One of the most important practices that you can acquire to build body heat and intuitive awareness is what I call "the body check." To properly do a body check, you need to direct your attention to your senses and experience them in greater depth and detail than you normally do. Doing this every so often will increase health, power, intuition, and your ability to use your intention to organize your environment telepathically. Without this kind of conscious awareness, your natural body heat gets lost in the many other senses that your target experiences. So practice being aware of the totality of you; this awareness will shift from moment to moment and reveal your profound capacity for change.

The body check will also help you know exactly who else is taking space within you. You didn't think that you were the only one sending and receiving body heat, did you? Consciously or unconsciously we are all sending one another telepathic messages all of the time. All someone really has to do is to think of you for more than a moment, and "zap!" Just like that, they are within you. As you practice the body check you will become aware of who is inside of you and what their agenda is, so that you will be able to decide whether or not you want them there at all. A warning: telepathy, especially BHT, can be very distracting. For example, someone might be pining away for you, sending you his feelings of sadness and nostalgia, which you then mistake for your own. Anger, worry, even memories—all of these things may take space where your own self and intention should reside.

Of course, we want some of this telepathy. I obviously want to know if my son is okay or how my partner is feeling—but only when I *need* to know. Inasmuch as it is important to understand the power of when to use telepathy, we must also understand when it can hurt us and how to protect ourselves from that kind of damage. The challenge is that we are always on automatic alert with the people we love or feel responsible toward. So the question begs: once we recognize the *unwanted* thoughts and feelings that others are sending to us, how do we keep them out? Believe me, you do not want to feel your fear response to your ex's anger all day, as it will obviously not help you function powerfully. You do not want to be part of your best friend's resentment, your sister's jealousy, your mother's disdain, or countless other messages that you might pick up. The only self-defense against unwanted telepathy is to fully embody your own reality.

Much of the awareness of what you need to struggle with—past, present, and future—comes to you when you embody your own reality. So you need to muster the courage to direct your intuition to integrate this information and commit all of your senses to resolving the "body snatchers" within yourself that inhabit places that could be more powerfully inhabited by different parts of you. It is a full sensory experience of your best self.

Riding public transportation is a really fun experiment in telepathy. Depending on whom you sit next to, your senses and thoughts will change. I really try to be physically close only to people who can transform me in positive ways. The only self-defense against unwanted telepathy is to embody your own reality. This is a more complex process than it seems at first. A lot of awareness of what you need to struggle with past, present, and future comes to your awareness when you embody. It is a full sensory experience of your best self and a consciousness of what is keeping you from your best self. This consciousness of both internal and external obstacles engages intuition to resolve them.

It is not particularly easy to maintain your focus of attention on your best self, but trust me when I tell you that it is a transformative and invaluable practice and can help you to understand your connectedness to everything around you, allowing you to create your own desired change. When you are feeling the invasion of the "body snatchers," it is the best time to make the effort. Think of it as an experience of fully inhabiting yourself so that there is no space for anything that does not serve your best interests. Once again, to be effective, this practice may not always be comfortable. When you embody your own reality, the first senses and memories that will come up will be the ones that you need to address in the moment, so that you can move to a fuller use of your own power and mastery of self. Allow these things to come up—don't try to avoid or repress them—and then put them aside. You may want to jot them down or take a deep breath and simply observe them passing through you like a small cloud in a blue sky. Sometimes the issue and its solution will reveal themselves simultaneously.

Body heat telepathy, using telepathy to ignite true, deep, enduring desire and commitment, has many unique components, in part because the telepathy we send and our receptors to the body heat telepathy of others were well developed before we were verbal, ambulatory beings—when we were just babies! The roots of what you find attractive and what attracts others to you is deeply instinctive and patterned so early in your life that transformation requires special attention and care to the most primal parts of your awareness. Also, the level and depth of connection that you want to intensify or uncover with a prospective romantic partner is much more intimate and risky and needs to be more viscerally satisfying than what you might want from a friend, business partner, or child. It is also equally important to know how to clear the deep, primal connections you have made in the past that may be distorting your ability to function in or attract a love relationship now. Again, remember that these connections are stored in a very deep and subconscious part of you, and it will take focus, practice, and consistent awareness to reform them.

True Love Awaits

Fact: there is true love for you. It does not matter how old you are, what your situation is, what you look like, or any physical, emotional, or spiritual damage you think you have. What does matter is which part of yourself you choose to experience and how you send it out into the world. In the process of learning how to "body-heat" your perfect world and draw love toward you, the real treasure will be that of finding your true, passionate, attractive self and the wholeness of your own heart.

I do not believe in soul mates (my sincere apologies to the hopeless romantics among you). More than once in my life I have been deeply in love and connected in a way that still remains and probably will remain forever. When we experience betrayal, loss, or change, we often decide that that person was not our soul mate. The truth is that there are many people in the world who are ideal for you, partners whose heart, values, personalities, and even genetics fit you in a way that makes them feel like family in the most transcendent and passionate way. That is why, once in a relationship, commitment and communication are important to nurture every day. There are thousands of second chances out there (and third and fourth and . . .) all of which may be soul mates. Often, your inner picture of who your soul mate is does not fit your true needs.

One of the loveliest surprises of being telepathically attuned is the ability to see the real and true inner beauty and sensuality that you would otherwise miss in others. Think back to high school: How many of the people who looked pretty turned into frogs later in life? How many people who were seen as duds are now superstars? There are so many treasures to be found when you look with your heart as well as your head, and the genuine treasure is the person who is able to find and appreciate the treasure in you. Much of what we look for in another person is not what will really connect us passionately and profoundly. It is simply a pattern stemming from the early expectations and judgments of others and our own wounded sense of self-worth. A relationship with "that person" from "that place" in you will not make you feel alive for long. Some of you will likely use body heat first to attract that fantasy relationship, the one that thrills and then ultimately disappoints. That is why I really want to stress the importance of healing your own heart through this process, of finding your own true inner heat, the heat and heart you want to live with *and* want to express in the world and with a partner.

The processes of healing and attraction are not sequential. You can begin them together, and a partner can help you move through the healing part. In fact, partners are each other's best healers if they use telepathy and body heat for that purpose. By working through this chapter as you are negotiating with each other all of the time, it is important not to jump into relationships that come your way immediately. You will instantly begin to attract people to you, but as you do, you need to check in regularly on your own healing. Be a connoisseur of the people you really let into your life. Take good care of your own precious heart.

How to Use Body Heat Telepathy

Here is how to use body heat telepathy on someone specific. We will call this person your "target" for the purpose of this exercise. Throughout the day there may be people you want to body-heat to make them more predisposed to you. We went over a more general use of telepathy in the previous chapter. Now we can explore how to influence just about anyone using your telepathic ability (in the form of body heat telepathy) and how to defend yourself against their telepathy by filtering which influences you want to let in, and when. For the purpose of this section, we will focus on love.

At this point you should have some basic sense of how it feels to feel your own body heat state in general. Now let us detail the heat for a specific person or target. As we stated earlier, the first step in tailoring body heat to a specific person or target is to allow a sense of what they, in the moment, need to feel from you to make you interesting to them.

Remember, you can't just imagine or invent a person you wish you were. You actually need to find this person within yourself—and believe wholeheartedly that this part of you exists. The tele-pathic dialogue you will engage in with your target happens from subconscious to subconscious, and if you're not attuned to your best self, their subconscious will pick up your telepathy as white noise that doesn't come from a genuine place in you. However, there are many places within you where you can find a true you that is in sync with what your target needs. But first you have to believe that you are a whole lot of people that you may never have met. Getting to know yourself, more of yourself, and the other parts of yourself are all part of the fun.

By doing the work in the first part of this chapter, your "radar" will be right on point. You won't be one of those people who does not see what is clear to everyone else, or whose attraction is guided by injured parts unknowingly seeking further injury. In my book *Welcome to Your Crisis,* I discuss a vitally important rule: no new damage. This rule applies during everyday life, as well as in times of crisis or dramatic changes. When you decide to make a change, you need more of your resources to be working effectively for you. The idea is to grow past old injury and be extremely wary of incurring any new damage. The challenge is that new damage is not always obvious. It could come in the form of having lunch with the person whom you see each month because you have been friends for decades, but who somehow always makes you feel powerless. It could be spending money that you don't have because you think new clothes will help you embody the new you. Whatever "it" may be, be aware and be wary, and do not add wood to a fire that is already hot. Ardently follow the rule, which I gratefully lifted from my psychiatrist, Dr. Frank Miller: No New Damage!

Now that your attention is on keeping yourself protected and centered in your wholeheartedness, let us return your attention to your target: the person you want to body-heat. Allow your attention to go to the other person. You don't have to look at him or her or even be close to him or her to do this. Simply experience your senses, thoughts, and feelings extending into the other person and then allow yourself to experience what the other person needs, wants, desires, what his or her love fantasy is, and what you have to offer that would meet that. You will feel, at first, that you are just imagining this information, but in time, as you move toward the core of your love truths, you will find that you extend your intuitive sensors toward the other person more easily and clearly, which poises you to receive the information you need each time. People always ask me, "How do you know it's intuitive information and not just something you have made up?" There are some ways you can know it's *not* intuitive, but the only way you know that it really *is* intuitive is if your information is genuine. The process of understanding how to separate the genuine needs from the artificial, requires time and repetition, as everyone always chalks their first success up to coincidence. Once again, start off by not questioning yourself. Just notice the senses that perk up, and try the Quick Hit exercise a few times. The result will prove itself.

When body-heating someone, it is important to keep your awareness both on the visceral sensation—the information-filled area between you and the target—as well as the ever-changing information about the other that you receive. You will be sending feelings, visual scenes, story lines, tastes, smells, and even movement. Everything a human being can sense is something that you may perceive about the other, feel within yourself, and send to the other. Let us do a practice example on paper.

Let's say you are in a coffee shop (cliché, I know, sorry). You see and sense someone who may be right for you. You do a quick check of the exercises in the first part of this chapter to make sure that you are not getting yourself into trouble (no new damage!). You ask yourself questions such as: Is he someone who fits my usual neurotic pattern? Is he my real love ideal?

If all systems are go, you switch your attention to what is going on inside of him, using the same technique that you used in chapter 1 on information gathering (intuition), but this time, with his love ideal as your target. The Quick Hit exercise on page 101 can guide you, but for our purposes here, practice doing it quickly—for example, at a party or meeting where many targets may be present. The idea is that you want to be able to figure out various peoples' love idea and merge the results into an attractive you as quickly as possible. You allow your senses to travel into the part of him that holds *his* love ideal, and if your attention is in place, your attention will find this place. It may all seem like haphazard information, but go with your intuition to know that there is some kind of greater picture taking shape. Here is one way it can go: Perhaps you get an image of a house in, say, Connecticut, and you think it may be where he grew up; you feel people laughing together, having their own lives but being aware of the strong base they share. Now you feel the ability to be part of this within yourself. Now you get a sense of his wanting someone who really supports his work, a real partner, and as you get this sense you also experience how he experiences sensuality, a welcoming ease, a delicious homecoming, lots of conversation, and easy physical contact. You get a picture of a big family and you insert yourself into this picture with pleasure. You find this person within yourself, and as you do so, you get the sense that he would be interested in the fact that you left a great job to start your own company. You are then struck by the sense that he loves adventure and wants to be more adventurous himself. You smell vanilla so you add that to your sensory body heat. And so on . . .

Now embody the person you have found within yourself who

122

fits his ideal. *Be* that person. You can use pieces of memories to do it or access the parts of you through feeling or any of your other senses that you believe represent his love ideal. Once you are really embodying this ideal, use all of your senses to make the connection from that person within you to the inside of him. Some of you may find that you "breathe" the sense over, while some of you may see the connection ride a color between the two of you. Some of you might get a hit of smell in the air between you, and some of you may simply feel the connection or "know" that it is there. Everyone is unique in how she uses her senses to experience intuition. You may find that you do not choose your typical modality. Those of you who tend to use sight might this time use scent. This is because you are intuitively using the target's modality of reception. Of course we all use them all at once (and should for a powerful body-heat send), but don't be surprised if you have a preference.

Once you have embodied the right body heat position and started the telepathic dialogue, you have two choices: one is to send and wait, the other is to send only when you sense the time is right for making contact. Keep in mind that your intuition will give you a lot of information that you didn't ask for but will still be useful to you as you make your decision to send or wait. Is this person in a relationship? How is he feeling in this moment? What would tantalize him as an opening line? And so on. Many solid relationships start as friendships and are built on understanding and patience until the "aha" moment comes along.

If you pick the second choice (and intuition will help guide you), you will want to use the target you have chosen to decide how to approach without breaking the body heat telepathic connection. However it occurs, once you make contact you will want to stay "in character" (i.e., tapped into your best self), which may take some practice.

You have done this before without realizing it. I, for example, have friends with whom I always use foul language. I also, however, have friends with whom a softer, more accommodating side of me emerges. Somehow or other, I always intuitively know which me to be. We have all unconsciously used body heat throughout our lives. I am showing you how to use it intentionally and with specific results.

Using Body Heat in an Existing Romantic Relationship

To use your body heat in an existing relationship you need to experience the other person as unconnected to you. You may want to place him in your mind's eye, somewhere in front of you at a distance. You need to imagine that you are not connected to the person in any way. Consider him a stranger, someone new to discover. Before we move to the next step, you need to reassure yourself of your ability to create change in the relationship. Some of what you intuitively pick up (in fact, probably most of it) will stir a reaction in you. You want to stay away from your reactions, which originate in your old connection to this person and how you *think* you want him to experience you and life with you. In short, try to be aware of how you tend to react to disturbing information and find something—a thought, an activity, a deep breath, *anything*—to short-circuit that reaction.

You then embody your state of wholeheartedness. I warn you

not to wander into step two of this exercise until you are firmly rooted in step one.

Now, allow your senses to extend into the other person. Find where he holds his current structure of love and desire. What is he longing for? What motivates him? Take time to allow the information to flow toward you. Keep your position of distance, even distanced from the information. Be close enough to register it but not close enough to react to it. You may get a flood of information or just a few bits, like "He wants someone who finds him funny" or "He doesn't want anything to change at all." Be careful that paranoia doesn't step in disguised as intuition to tell you, "He's fooling around" or "He doesn't love me anymore."

Usually what you are afraid to find is not intuitive information but some kind of emotional projection. The same thing goes for what you know you *want* to find. You should be careful of both wishes *and* fears when you are performing body heat telepathy. You intuitively know what most of these are. Put them aside, as they will not help you achieve your goal. As you do this you will get very detailed information about the parts of you that need to be strengthened in this relationship and those that need to be tempered. Perhaps you will need to work through a part of yourself that you are afraid of and have kept hidden for years. Many new possibilities for change will emerge, and you will have the opportunity to use them for transformation, not only for the relationship, but even more important, for yourself.

Okay, now what about your goals? You may first want to do some exploratory telepathy to gauge your reactions and interest and clarify what it is you really want. If you are not getting what you really want in a relationship where you once did, chances are that there is also a part of you that is conflicted as to whether or not you want this person or like who he has become. Even if your conscious feeling is one of wanting to hold on, start to listen more carefully to the part of you that may not want to but is doing so out of fear or inner injury. It is important to sort this out before you start the process of body heat. Much of the process of body heat and telepathy may have been clarified for you in the first part of this chapter. Some of you may not understand right away, and instead, an understanding will evolve over time and your changes in behavior and attention will guide you. Notice what *you* are doing, thinking, feeling. As you receive some information and are able to shift internally, you will get more information and, in turn, make more shifts. Sometimes you don't know where you will end up. Know that you will be safe because you are consciously directing this evolution toward a wholehearted relationship and a self-healed heart.

Eventually your goal will become clear. You may use body heat to put passion back into a relationship or to express needs and motivate behaviors in the other person, with whom you have been unsuccessful in achieving traditional dialogue or actions. When your goal is clear, your body heat telepathy will be its most effective, as you will be using all of your intention and energy in a single direction.

I remember a student who made a love wish for someone new because her current relationship was not working out. She did the healing and the body heat telepathy and was surprised to find that it was not someone new that came into her life but the old relationship now healed. She then shifted her body heat to continue to create the relationship she wanted with this man, day

to day, moving forward. As I said earlier, we are all always changing, and the ability to be responsive to change as well as become
the catalyst for change is key to a vibrant relationship—in fact,
to a vibrant and joyful life.

The best time to body-heat someone close to you is, oddly,
not when you are with them physically. In their presence the best
use of your senses is to engage fully with the other person in an
interactive, immediate way. The best time to use body heat is in
moments of wholeness and calm.

You will find that your body heat telepathy with your partner
will allow you to make subtle changes that both of you respond
to in a positive way. A warning about body heat and your partner:
you are already deeply enmeshed with your partner in a way that
you would not be with a person you haven't yet met or shared
time with. In all relationships there are some areas where you
project things onto the other partner that are really more about
you. It is a bit like two different-color threads being woven into
the same carpet so tightly that it is hard to see which thread is
which. Extra time and attention needs to be given to your own
internal changes as you body-heat an existing relationship. In
most relationships, especially marriages, each person wants to
have a relationship with the person they are married to, but not
the kind of relationship they are currently having, which is starv-
ing them, depressing them, or limiting them in some other way.
It is not the person who is wrong, but what the relationship has
become. This can often be healed through body heat telepathy.

How do you know the relationship is being healed? Because
as you will see, it will begin to improve and stay on that path of
positive evolution. There are, of course, always bumps; but the

key is to look at the sum total of, say, a month, and then be able to say, "Yes, we are in a much better place as a couple than we were a month ago."

When a partner doesn't change, it can mean one of a few things: he won't, he is not ready to, or simply he cannot evolve. If the latter is true, chances are that your own work on yourself will have already given you lots of information and healing guidance to help you accept a "can't" from your partner. Your body heat telepathy has already begun to bring love and healing into your life. If and when your partner is ready, he will respond to it, too, if the match is right for you. If not, it will help you attract the love and support to leave.

In any situation, body heat telepathy engages both you and your target toward awareness and change. In a sense, you are always experiencing it *with* someone, not performing it *on* someone. You get more engaged with the person as you create the conditions for him to become more engaged with you. You do not want to perform body heat on someone whom you are trying to leave. All it does then is muddy the waters.

Using Body Heat in Nonromantic Relationships

Many of you have relationships that you have entertained for a long time—lovers, family, friends—many of which may not be in the optimal state. In romantic scenarios, people tend to think that the natural progression of a relationship is toward a comfortable stasis, a balance that no longer has much "juice." This is a dangerous concept, since we know that we are all changing in every moment. The upside of this fact is that every moment is also an opportunity to change. Even balance is a state of constant change, requiring the dynamic adjustment and readjustment of the people in a relationship.

Now we are going to focus on how to re-energize a relationship using your body heat telepathy. The interesting benefit in using this technique is that if the relationship cannot be re-energized, you will receive the clarity that you need to step back with confidence.

Relationships that last over time acquire their own unique persona. There are two people (more if there are children) together who form the relationship, as well as each of these people on their own, as individuals. The relationship, or family, actually has a character of its own that may not accurately reflect the people in it. This composite and often stagnant relationship doesn't always mean that the people in it are close. In fact, it is often quite the opposite. They cease to see each other as unique individuals, ready for discovery, and instead fall into patterns, which become uninteresting and lacking in heat, until an outside influence shakes one of them up. You can also lose your individual qualities to the "relationship" and forget they are yours. The relationship makes you successful, the relationship makes you depressed, or the relationship makes you safe or unsafe. A good relationship continues to be an active negotiation between its individuals, who make choices every day to work on themselves and the way they interact in the framework of the relationship. If not, the relationship persona takes over, sucking the life out of its hosts.

But how do you reheat a relationship? The first requirement is distance. It doesn't have to be a physical distance, but instead, some kind of metaphoric, visceral space that you take. The distance needs to be a sensory untangling of the "us" of the relationship and a new awareness of two distinct people, in all of his or her individual complexity. Of course, if you have done the exercises in the first part of this chapter you already have a sense of your own complexity and the powerful parts of you that need your focus for success. Now you need to do the exercises in the first part of this chapter on the other person. Answer the same questions for him. He may not be ready or willing to shift to a healthier version of himself; however, information in hand, you can embody the parts of yourself that both engage and heal him.

The desire of all parts of a human being is to be whole. If you are working from your wholeheartedness *you* will be the guiding energy, the captain of the healing. This is never a smooth process. I have not once seen someone embody another's wholeness and then address it with immediate results. The injured part always kicks up some dust first. Remember, the injured part was once part of a real armor of protection for the person. It will not disappear without some convincing and time.

Warning Lights for Body Heat

While we are on the topic of using body heat on existing relationships, I offer you a word of caution: you probably shouldn't body-heat your ex. This is a relationship you want to disengage from so that you can reclaim parts of yourself, and depending on the length and intensity of the relationship, this process can take decades. You may not want to body-heat someone who has just rejected you even if you long for him, until you first do a bit of self-healing. After all, you definitely do not want to find yourself in the same situation yet again (no new damage).

As a matter of fact, you can use body heat in reverse to re-claim your lost parts. As we discussed, in a relationship, the bond itself becomes a person, and in leaving said relationship, you often have to separate shared parts of you from that relationship persona. I can't tell you how many times I have heard things like "Without her no one will love me" or "Without him I won't be able to pay my bills" or "She is the smart one" or "He made me happy." You need to take back all of those parts of you that were absorbed by the relationship persona, and body heat telepathy can help you do it. You need to body-heat yourself, as if you were a separate person. Really get to know you from arm's length and then charm yourself. You will get to know a version of yourself who may have been lost or never had a chance to develop in your old relationship. Breakups give us a chance to find the self that grew up during the relationship and now belongs to us. We learn from each other. It is important not to leave the learning in the relationship persona, or you will either repeat the same problem-atic relationship or find yourself unable to move on.

Body heat telepathy creates a relationship between two people even if they have yet to speak to each other, or even meet. You send information, but believe me when I say that just as much information and influence flows right back at you. Of course, I assume that if you are body-heating someone, you probably want that connection with him.

One of the biggest concerns about the concept of body heat telepathy is that it is manipulative. Well . . . it is. However, you are making a conscious choice to create a relationship with another person and explore his willingness to do so. We do this without being aware that we are doing it all of the time, often to the wrong people and often ineffectively and disruptively. It is much gentler on everyone to target people you really want in a way that makes them experience the very best, most wholehearted parts of themselves, and helps them direct those parts toward you—as opposed to shooting out body heat all over the place, never getting what you want, and disturbing the equilibrium of others.

When you body-heat consciously, it actually changes both you and the person you are body-heating. You need to reach for parts of yourself that you have never consciously met, as well as knowing the other person from the inside out. You notice when you target someone whom you shouldn't target (part of your old, halfhearted story), and ultimately, your awareness creates inner change. We are all deeply interconnected, which is why telepathy is so simple to learn and effective to use. As you practice your body heat telepathy, you will find that you feel some connection to everyone and a deep connection to some people, and have the ability to express yourself and make an impression without saying a word.

As a last note I would like to speak to *body heat and synchronicity*. Synchronicities are those meaningful coincidences in our lives that seem to come out of the blue. You may find that when you body-heat someone, you later run into him or her by "chance" a day, a month, or a year later. You may have even forgotten that you body-heated someone in the first place. You may feel an instant connection—he may end up being the right person at the right time. Synchronicity makes sense of your seemingly failed efforts. Synchronicity is one of life's ways of making sure we end up where we want and need to be. Keep track of your efforts and their results over time and you will be astounded by the power of your own whole heart.

Do not be surprised if after doing these exercises a few times you "coincidentally" find resolutions with people and in situations that once seemed intractable. People may notice you in a new way, respond to you differently, and things and people whom you once found acceptable or even attractive may be revealed anew. Telepathy is a powerful and natural innate ability, just like your ability to love and be loved in return.

If you do the suggested exercises, along with recording/documenting the results, you will set your communication toward your conscious goals, instead of allowing yourself to be guided by your unconscious ones. Patterns will be dissolved, desires uncovered, conflicts made conscious and then resolved and/or evolved. Of course the desired ultimate result is that your conscious and unconscious goals become one, and that you become at peace with yourself, working effectively to achieve all of your goals, creating and healing relationships that bring you effortless joy and let you know what you want and how to make it all happen in harmony. You are communicating right now with the people you love, have loved, and will love. Each time you practice body heat telepathy you will communicate more effectively in a way that not only brings you love but uncovers the most precious love of all: the love you have for your authentic and unique self.

Repatterning Your Love Code
with Daily Processes

Simple awareness is a powerful tool. Allow your intuition to give you a memory of a moment when you loved with your whole heart. It may have been a person, a pet, a stuffed animal, or even an idea. Take a moment to experience that moment of love again. It doesn't matter how that moment ended. What matters is the reminder of loving with your whole and open heart. The first part of this chapter is designed to open up new parts of yourself so that you can use body heat effectively, powerfully, and safely. You have already completed stage one.

I have asked you to answer, for yourself, some difficult questions, and simply being aware of the answers has brought you and will continue to bring you to a new state of being and your birthright of a whole heart. I want to say here that it may not be that your parents didn't *want* to love you. They were, perhaps, too damaged to be able to love completely. Maybe their own upbringing or societal expectations made it hard for them to accept who you were, so that their "love" consisted of loving an idealized image of you or rejecting parts of you that composed who you really were and are. I believe that, mostly, people do the best that they can with what they have to work with, which is why I am devoted to creating tools for choice.

I want to speak for a moment about what I will call your "resting body heat position." This is your personal embodiment, which we worked on in the first part of this chapter, the notion of being wholehearted. It is who you are when you are loved, lovable, and in love with yourself. This is a healing place to rest in throughout the day. It helps your body and brain do the things you need to do to physically, emotionally, and intellectually heal from the unhealthy patterns of the past. Whenever you have a moment, and especially when things are going badly, this is when your attention and senses should seek your resting body heat position. This will not always be easy to achieve, but the more you embody your whole heart, the easier it will be to access this state in times of stress. Throughout your day, find that place and person within yourself and seek the thoughts, memories, and feelings that inspire you to be wholehearted.

Here are some additional insights, meant to be explored every few days or so. It takes time to integrate new information so that it feels familiar. Give yourself the time.

Body Heat Telepathy Process 1:
Daily Chats to Engage Myself and My Intuition

- These are the parts of me that I feel/have been told are lovable: _____

    _____

    _____

    _____

- These are the parts of me that I feel/have been told are unlovable: _____

    _____

    _____

    _____

- The adults in my childhood loved me because I was

  _____

  _____

  _____

  _____

- These are the things that I did and became to keep their
  love: _____

  _____

  _____

  _____

- This is what I am realizing the adults around me have
  taught me about love: _____

  _____

  _____

  _____

- What do I fear about being in a mutually passionate,
  loving, supportive relationship? (If you can't think of
  anything here, make something up. If there were no fears,
  you would be in the relationship already. You may need
  to use intuition and imagination to get yourself going.)

  _____

  _____

  _____

  _____

- Now that I am wiser, how can I choose to view what I was loved for and who I was in the past that makes me lovable to myself now? _____

  _____

  _____

  _____

- This is how I choose to love and be loved: _____

  _____

  _____

  _____

  _____

- This is what I think I want or need in a partner and why (this will evolve as you do these exercises): _____

  _____

  _____

  _____

  _____

- After looking at the last list, this is what I really want and need in a partner (let this flow out of you): _____

  _____

  _____

  _____

  _____

  _____

Body Heat Telepathy Process 2:
Vestigial Self

Explore these concepts by writing about them in your journal.

- These are the selves within me who do not help me attract love, express love, trust, or be discerning in love. These selves have a history. When were they born? Who or which experiences steered their development? These are the messages that I send out subliminally, through my thoughts, expectations, and feelings that may be off-putting to the love I want to attract: _____

  _____

  _____

  _____

  _____

  _____

  _____

- These are the memories or fantasies that I can feel and believe with all of my senses to send out telepathy of attraction: _____

  _____

  _____

  _____

  _____

  _____

• What patterns have I habitually formed in relationships?

_____

_____

_____

_____

• This is the mini ritual I am going to do throughout the day to pattern my wholehearted body heat into my subconscious habits. (It can be writing, deep breathing exercises, or simply walking alone outside; these little rituals will help you formalize the repatterning process):

_____

_____

_____

_____

• These are the ways that I have found to help me re-experience my resting body heat state. I am reminding myself of them so that I can use them throughout the day (you may want to make up short code words for these things as you go along): _____

_____

_____

_____

• Today I noticed that my body heat had an effect on the following people: _____

_____

_____

- Today I noticed that my body heat had an effect on the following situations: _____

_____

_____

_____

- The body heat I did another day paid off today in the following way: _____

_____

_____

_____

- Today, this is what it feels like to be wholehearted:

_____

_____

_____

_____

- As I change and heal every day I need to remind myself of who I am today. Today, I am _____

_____

_____

_____

Body Heat Telepathy Process 3:
Repatterning Your Love Code at Night

It is helpful to do repatterning at night so that intuition and memory can find the solutions and help you make important emotional and behavioral shifts as you sleep. During the day all of your resources are directed toward responding to your thoughts and environment. At night, you have full access to yourself to engage in other tasks. It is important to choose the tasks you do at night so that you wake up ready to achieve your goals.

Before you go to sleep you need to perform a ritual to represent what it is you are trying to achieve with your body heat telepathy. This ritual should have real meaning for you and use your natural talents. Do the ritual after reviewing the information that you received from your own intuition and subconscious in the first part of this chapter. You may want to adjust this information as your life changes, as it will if you practice body heat telepathy consistently.

A ritual can be as simple as holding a piece of jewelry you wear every day to your heart before you go to sleep, feeling the strength of your heartbeat as you do it, and giving yourself the gentle suggestion that as you sleep you will reap all the wisdom from your dreams. The next morning, you might place this "protector" on your body to keep you centered in your own body heat throughout the day. You can touch the item when you feel stressed or lost or need guidance. This is just one example. I have a little table in my room where I write down my struggles, and I place the notes under a shell I found on the beach. I then put my jewelry on the table and I sometimes light a candle and allow the flame to guide me as I gaze at it. I have photos of things and people I love on the table and around it. I change it as I change. When I place my jewelry on my body, I bless myself with the power I have given it. You need to be consistent so that you do not fall into old behavioral patterns but instead continue to make your life and love better and stronger every day. One step forward, one step back is an exhausting way to live.

Now, back to your ritual. Your nightly ritual should be quick and simple, or you will be unlikely to continue it over time. If you are an artist, it can include a quick sketch of you and your love in an embrace; if you are spatially oriented, you may want to place two similar objects closer and closer together each night. If you are a writer, you may want to write a quick love poem expressing you and your lover's feeling for each other. You may want to put on your nightly cream imagining your lover's hands touching your face. Your ritual should be simple and consistent. Your feelings and perceptions will change each time you do your ritual, depending on which part of your internal process and obstacles you will be working through that night. You won't really know the "why" of the change until the morning, or until you see the change in your life. Go with whatever you are experiencing and suspend judgment, as much as you are able, and don't feel the need to know how well you are doing it or how far along you are. It is important that you perform the same ritual each night, as it is a cue for your subconscious and your telepathy to repattern themselves to love and be loved.

This will naturally lead you to a smaller version of this ritual that you can do as a subconscious pattern affirmation during the day. It may be as simple as looking at a picture that you have put on your key ring or repeating a phrase a few times while feeling your resting body heat state. The intricacies of the ritual are not important. Its meaning to you holds its real power.

Before you go to sleep at night, very briefly (did I mention that these exercises should be very, very brief?) run through the information you received from your intuition during the exercises in the first part of this chapter, allowing yourself to be aware of new information as it comes in. You do your body heat ritual and then, as you go to sleep, you embody your true love next to you and, picking from your intuitive/memory file, you embody and experience as fully as you are able a you that both your partner and your self can love and have a wonderful, passionate, joyful relationship with. Don't worry about the sensory noise that gets in the way: "There isn't really anyone with me, I am alone. Will I always be alone? I am too old, or skinny, or fat, or stupid, etc." Don't try to repress these sensory blips. Repression gives them more power; simply practice bringing your focus back to your beloved and your being loved. Breathing helps. We often hold our breath when we have a thought, a sense, or feeling that upsets us. Just breathe. Allow yourself to experience as much of your body and as many of your senses as you are able. Allow yourself to experience as much of the other person as you are able. Connect to this person, even if he doesn't exist in your life yet, and allow him to connect to you. Sleep in the person's arms. Allow your senses to be as rich and real as you can. Of course your mind will wander, just as it would if you were in the flesh, lying with this person, falling asleep. Don't worry about the distractions—instead, focus on the telepathy, confident that you are doing it right.

When you awaken in the morning, jot down any dreams or awareness that you may have woken with. This has two purposes. The first one is to allow yourself to tune in to some of the valuable work you did during the night, even if it doesn't make sense to you immediately. The second one is to allow yourself to shift from whatever state you awakened in to a state of body heat. You set your attraction telepathy to "on." I am sure that by now you are getting some feeling about the attractive you. Practice being in that you all day by shifting your feelings, thoughts, reactions, and memories in a way that you can actually experience the wholehearted you. Many of you have had the experience of being in love, and the telepathy of love and fulfillment is so strong that everyone crawls out of the woodwork to be near you. Then, when love fades and you are feeling abandoned and unlovable, this magical attraction disappears. This is the power of body heat telepathy.

CHAPTER 6

Remote Viewing

We all sit around in a circle and suppose, while the secret sits in the center and knows.

—ROBERT FROST

Quick Hit Exercise for Remote Viewing

Use a pad to write down notes or sketch drawings for the following exercise:

1. Choose your target—in this case, a physical destination.

2. Assume that you are there, body and mind.

3. Assume that all of your perceptions and experiences are taking place in your destination.

4. Document what and whom you notice in detail. The images may be fragmentary or complete. Don't limit yourself to what you see, but include what your other senses are also picking up.

What You Experienced in the Quick Hit

Whatever you noticed, even if it seemed to be a simple awareness of your environment—such as the phone ringing, or some vague feeling of nothingness—*anything* that you noticed began to build the target in your awareness. The more detailed your documentation, the more clearly you were able to define your target. Some of the building blocks may have been symbols or metaphors, and some were direct experiences as read by your senses. As you practice, you will view your target and its environment more literally and in more detail. You may not have observed your target from the ground up. You may have pieced it together: a corner here, an impression there, a looming sense of something. The way you built your target is probably the way you address your life. Did you go in through the back door? Did you stay outside or above it? More than any other Quick Hit in this book, this exercise will tell you how you interact with the structures in your life.

What Is Remote Viewing?

Whereas **telepathy** is all about finding areas of attachment, **remote viewing** is one of the most detached intuitive states. By the way, the viewing we speak of is not always visual. People who do not "see" images view through any and all of their other senses the same way they would experience any new environment. In remote viewing, you are able to assess the framework of a place or situation with great equanimity. It is the least reactive form of intuitive work. It is also a good organizational tool to use when placing information obtained through your other intuitive senses (as well as any other kind of data) into a framework. Although many intuitive skills require you to retain a detached perspective, you enter remote viewing through the perception of physical structures separate from and alien to you; more than any other kind of intuitive skill, it tends to keep its perspective throughout. When remote viewing loses perspective, it becomes astral projection, which we will also cover in this chapter.

YOU CAN USE REMOTE VIEWING IN COUNTLESS WAYS:

- To find the strengths or weaknesses in any structure, body, or process

- To participate remotely in situations

- To view a meeting that you were not invited to

- To locate a missing person or object

- To view relationships

- To project development

- To evaluate real estate in terms of both structure and neighborhood

- To solve problems with structure or engineering

- To view competitors' products or strategies

- To evaluate your own products or strategies

- To visit scenes from your past or your family's past and view them with new eyes

- To explore archaeology

- To locate oil, precious metals, or anything else that is hidden to the naked eye

- To plan investments

- To view a strategy as a whole

- To determine the purpose or functionality of a physical location

- To address multicomponent strategies

- To evaluate, with precognition, all of these things in the future and come up with effective strategies for change

- To view the end result of a project

- To view market readiness or market needs

. . . and many other things that you will come up with based on your needs.

Remote viewing allows you to travel not just through space, but also through time. You can view something as it is now, but you can also view a building as it will be built when it is finished (useful for troubleshooting in advance) or your mother's childhood bedroom (perhaps helpful to come up with the perfect sixtieth birthday gift). Usually, when you decide to view a location without stipulating the exact time, you will experience the "seeing" as it is in the exact moment that you are doing the exercise. This often happens in your sleep state when something is going on that you need to know about in a remote location.

The fact is, you are visiting other places all the time, but you may not be aware of it. In fact, notice when someone tells you about a building they are buying, a company they are setting up, or an investment strategy they are planning. Chances are that your attention goes automatically to what stands out about the situation they are structuring, be it positive or negative. The next time someone tells you a story about a place they have visited, notice the pictures, sounds, and other sense impressions you get of the place as they tell you the story. Be aware of your changing body sensations—changes in temperature, scent, sound, feeling, and even what you taste in your mouth. If you carry a little notepad like I do, you can discreetly jot things down. If you know the person talking to you well enough that they will not think you're crazy (or if they already accept that you are), report these impressions to them. You will find that you remote-view automatically all of the time. As with all of your intuitive abilities, until you learn to direct remote-view, it gets lost in your other mental/perceptual activities. It also is easily misdirected by your subconscious or your curiosity to places that are not worth remote viewing, not useful, or even borderline traumatic. When you master remote viewing, it becomes yet another useful tool with which to direct your life.

Déjà vu is part of our daily lives. Everyone can relate to the experience of walking into a new place or situation and feeling a familiarity, maybe even a foreknowledge of the situation. If your sense of déjà vu—spontaneous, precognitive remote viewing—is functioning in a healthy way, you will be able to preview situations that you need to prepare for but are not yet consciously aware of, often ones that involve what would otherwise lead to some level of traumatic shock. Your sleep state is often used for this function, allowing you to accept, process, prepare for, and even avoid a future event, so that you can respond effectively in a situation where you might have responded reactively, and perhaps to your detriment, had you not experienced the location or event in the first place. Can you remember a time when you didn't just *know* but actually *saw* a friend in trouble, or a store without your product, or a closet without your boyfriend's clothes in it? All of this is remote viewing. How do you know that you are viewing a location and not just making it up? Once again, you can never be sure until you verify your information against fact; however, in the case of remote viewing, you will tend to be surprised by what you see. It is rarely what you "thought," and by the time you begin to focus on it and get the conscious information to document it, your subconscious already has a pretty good grasp on it, rarely feeling surprised even when you believe it should.

Oftentimes, your spontaneous incidents of remote viewing occur when loved ones or personal property is threatened. I was riding in a car on the way to my country house on my birthday. I was in a great mood, just enjoying the ride and the conversations around me. All of a sudden I became panicked about my cat, whom I had left in the country the day before. I couldn't get my attention off him. Instinctively I looked for him in my mind's eye and didn't see him in the house where he, an indoor cat, was supposed to be. I felt so cold, even in the heated car. I was in a state of panic until I arrived at my front door. Sure enough, the house had been robbed; many of the sliding doors had been left open and the cat had run off. I was already so familiar with the picture of the burglarized house that by the time I arrived I barely noticed that the television and stereo were gone. I looked for my cat, first in my mind's eye and then when I had a sense of where he was—safe—I found him by shaking a box of dry cat food in the woods.

If you look up "remote viewing" on search engines you will find the discussions overrepresented by scientists, PhDs, and universities (Princeton and Stanford, to name two), as compared to discussions of other intuitive skills. Even the federal government put tens of millions of dollars into research on remote viewing in the 1970s. I believe that this is because it can be tested in a very methodical way, it has clear military applications, and (unlike some of the other tools we explore in this book) you won't feel like a complete wacko asking for funding to research it. It's kind of the "Rambo" area of intuitive skills.

One way that remote viewing has been tested is to set a computer to randomly generate an image at some future time that provides the answer to a question. One image, for example, is assigned to the market going up, one image to the market going down. The remote viewer then predicts not whether or not the market will go up or down but which image the computer will generate, representing the correct answer in the future, say, in exactly ten minutes. The viewer then describes or, most commonly, sketches the object intuitively. The image that the viewer sketches is the answer to the question.

There are many long, complicated courses available to train remote viewing, but I find that my students can do this with little or no training (and they are representative of the general population, as I teach many nonbelievers from companies where the CEO makes them attend my lectures, as well as regular people who cannot normally find their own keys). Don't overcomplicate a simple skill. As with anything else in life, remote viewing is not always 100 percent accurate or totally comprehensive. There is a lot to be said for beating the odds.

I had a dear friend, Hella Hammid, now of blessed memory. She was one of the subjects in the Stanford Research Institute experiments in the 1970s, one of the many university studies on the capacities of the human mind. She could view remote locations with great accuracy (which you can all do, by the way). What made Hella unique as a remote viewing subject was that she could draw what she saw so precisely. She was a visual artist and a well-known photographer, and this ability helped her express what she "saw" as a viewer.

You may be able to describe the location in accurate detail and you may also get symbols (as Hella did once, drawing a nuclear reactor as a boiling tea kettle) to describe what you are seeing. As you become aware that you are using a symbol to represent an object, the next time you see the same symbol you will know what object or target it represents. This awareness most often happens when an item/image/idea disturbs you in its regular form—say, a nuclear reactor or another woman with your husband. You may also perceive something that symbolizes the meaning of what you are viewing. An interviewer on a talk show I was on, for example, who has a very unpleasant love life and a public romance with food, "viewed" a heart that I had placed in a box as "something having to do with food." If you want to focus on getting the literal objects, people, and events in the place you view, you'll need lots of practice and repetition. It is also helpful to sketch out what you "see." Even if you are as terrible an artist as I am, the exercise will help you focus more clearly on form, placement, and what is really, physically going on in an area. Sketching out what you see and even including words and figures you feel like drawing but cannot identify is a way of getting more information before your conscious mind has time to recognize what place it is.

Allow yourself to use your remote viewing in whatever way

you are able. If you use it, it will develop into a skill with many applications in your daily life. I know that it is hard not to judge the quality of your information when you feel that you have missed your target, or not represented it literally, or allowed yourself to document only a little information. We are all built and hard-wired differently. You do not fail at remote viewing because you do not "see" literally. You may be someone who experiences the world in feelings and other descriptive senses, as well as symbols. Make the effort to understand the information you perceive as correct before you beat yourself up for being off. You will lose a lot of very good information if you don't give your own descriptive powers a chance. Some of you will get symbols at first, not the clarity and contrast that remote viewing allows.

One thing that I am sure of is that you are learning and developing this tool in the best way for your particular makeup. There are times when I will go from literal visions to symbols and not know why my subconscious is guiding my intuition to make that shift (or vice versa). I have learned to just go with whatever is happening, knowing that the explanation for why it has come to me in an unusual or circuitous way may not come until much later, if at all. I want my information to be useful, not overwhelming and not damaging. There are situations that we can see that would not be useful to see and would in fact be devastating.

Often, as with other intuitive abilities, you will only recall your remote viewing (or recognize what it was representing if you keep a journal) after the event. For many New Yorkers this was true of 9/11. They found themselves more prepared and less surprised than the situation would warrant and were therefore empowered to deal with the event as an effective community.

There are many stories amid the tragic, heartbreaking events, of people who just decided not to go to work that day or saw themselves to safety right before the planes hit.

Because of the detached nature of remote viewing (with emphasis on the word *remote*), it is often good to use this technique in situations that are emotionally charged, or where you may have a strong reaction to the information you seek. Certainly when making contact with traumatic moments from the past, or those that have the potential to traumatize you again, remote viewing is a safe choice. The same is true for the future. Whereas all of the other intuitive techniques to some degree welcome a firsthand, interactive experience, remote viewing will let you document the organization of something, and get the useful information to prepare for it, without having to get overly involved with the subject in an intricate way. Remote viewing allows perceptions with the boundary of structure.

Throwing You into the Deep End

You can view anything, from any perspective, at any point in time. You don't have to believe me on this one, just try it out for yourself. Do you know a friend who is renovating? "View" their completed home and compare notes with them. Describe the friend's childhood home to them and then look at pictures.

Now, think of a friend with whom you will speak within the next twenty-four hours. Write down the exact time and date. Now, find her with your attention. The same way you follow a thought or memory, go search for the person until you find her. This should take all of a second. How do you know you have found her? Until you have done this a few times, just give yourself thirty seconds and then assume that your impression is where she is.

Now, take a moment to notice what she is wearing, where she is, what is around her, who is around her, and what is going on. Stroll around and let your attention jump from one thing to another, documenting without analyzing. Then, document your hits and misses by verifying any accuracies and inaccuracies.

One of my favorite exercises to do with my students is to invite them into my home, without having them leave their seats. It is a quick visit with little preparation. Why don't we do this together now? Don't judge yourself on the basis of this exercise. Just use it as a warm-up and enjoy it. I think there is a bit of a voyeur in all of us. I want to invite you into my apartment in Rome, Italy. I don't want you to make this into some difficult, cerebral exercise. Just assume that you are there. Now walk around.

Now if you go through my apartment trying to guess what is there or figure out whether what you are experiencing or reacting to is real, you will inevitably get caught in your head. However, if you use your curiosity, your sensations, and your preferences to get really interested in my apartment in Rome, you will experience it easily. Touch things, open drawers, taste a little something from the kitchen. Look into anything and everything, even without my permission!

You don't even have to focus on doing this. Assume you are in my Rome apartment reading this book, answering a phone call, or balancing your checkbook. You can't force yourself to remote-view; you simply need to allow it to happen. Your attention will be someplace in your life and then, all of a sudden it will be in my Rome apartment, then back to your life. As you become accustomed to remote viewing, you will be more and more able to stay in a remote location without distracting yourself, but for now, it is more important to integrate it into your normal thinking process, easily and organically.

What do you notice about my Rome apartment? Did you go right into my apartment, or did you have to go up the stairs or ride the elevator to get there? What do you like, dislike? Take your time wandering around. For the sake of accuracy and simplicity, let's have you walk around my Rome apartment as it was on August 25, 2008. This way I can describe to you exactly what it looked like. Now I will, of course, omit many details that you may notice, but I will remark on the things where your attention is most likely to go. My apartment is only nine hundred square feet, not too big to see it all. Just jot down all that you "view," even if it doesn't make sense to you or fit the exercise.

Now let me describe my Rome apartment on August 25, 2008. It is on the fifth floor, with open tile stairs leading up and a tiny wooden keyed elevator. You walk in through a big brown door, where you see pink stucco walls and arches. The floor of the room you walk into is made of wood. In front of you is a frosted glass door, which leads to the kitchen and is often left open with the kitchen visible from the front door. To the right is a little bedroom with white marble floor tiles and a very colorful bedspread. If you pass that room, farther right you will find the living room. It is Turkish in style, also with pink stucco walls, and features a huge bedlike couch (you see I am hung up on couches) with a vibrant multicolored cover and loads of pillows (in fact, every area of my home is replete with pillows). There is a small television next to it and a pink couch facing it. There is a large, dark wooden desk, along with a white marble table. The windows in all of the rooms are mostly large and let in a lot of light.

As you walk in my kitchen door you see white wooden cabinets rimmed in light blue, gray marble counters, and cook surfaces with white tiles that feature large sunflowers on them. To the left of my entry there is a wall, then a storage closet, and then, farther left, is a large bedroom. The bedcover is blue and white, which is the basic color scheme of the room, including the drapes. There are white cabinets in every bedroom, including this one. There is a dark wood dresser with some bottles on top. The top of the dresser is black marble. The walls of both bedrooms are white. The bathroom is next to this room and has white tiles with a delicate blue pattern. You may note the following things in my apartment: There is a combination of old and new (I have had it for almost three decades and I am not good at cleaning out closets). There are framed posters of cats everywhere. The apartment is dotted with books. There is a little balcony with lights. When you look out from the balcony you see rooftops. The apartment is often empty of people. There are many memories there. There is quite a collection of my son's toys and games from more than a decade ago. We all tend to live and sleep in the living room when we are there. There are very soft fabrics, all kinds of silks, cashmere, and great sheets. Directly beneath me lives my dearest friend and neighbor of nearly thirty years, Fernanda. The roof is above me, where people hang their laundry. From my tiny balcony, which runs the length of the apartment, I can see everyone else's balcony, laundry hanging, a fruit store, a coffee bar, and many rooftops. My neighborhood is full of diverse ethnicities and little shops. The streets have few trees and are kind of gray.

Of course, you may have noticed a whole set of correct details that I forgot to mention, but you get the basic idea, right? If you allow this to be easy, it will be. Some areas of confusion with remote viewing are as follows: often, as you are experiencing the physical layout of a location, you will also perceive other information such as events that took place there, its history or future, and so on. Learning to hit and describe your target accurately is an ongoing challenge, and you can improve this skill over time.

As with other intuitive practices, because you can "time travel" it can be important to know at what point in time you are viewing your target. Let us speak for a moment about defining your target or destination. You can go anywhere with your attention. At times you will experience being in the location as if you really are there, and at times you will experience it more as a mental exercise. This often depends on your level of interest in the location or the people in it. It also depends on who you are. Some of you are more intellectual, some more sensory in your intuitive abilities. The time that you give yourself to view a location also determines to some extent the quality of your experience and its sensory load. If you have to get the information quickly, or if you have your curiosity sated right away, you will tend to experience the scene in less detail. You can even view a hypothetical, like your future hotel room or the dorm room your child will get next year.

Here is a little remote viewing exercise the government liked. I am going to give you some map coordinates. Go to that location through remote viewing and describe what is there. You can sketch it first if you wish and then add verbal detail so that you experience it from a few perspectives. Don't make this a long, drawn-out experience; you won't enjoy it that way. Do it quickly, without preparation, and assume that you know what is there. Follow your senses, all of your senses, and what they notice, even your thoughts. It is helpful to draw, feel temperature, describe feeling, notice structures, listen to sound, and so on. Document everything. Remember, if you don't "see" anything, you have other ways of knowing.

Go ahead, give it a shot. Here are the coordinates: latitude, 48 degrees, 51 minutes north; longitude, 2 degrees, 17 minutes east. The description of the location is on the bottom of page 175 with some of the hits you may have viewed.

Using Remote Viewing in Your Daily and Business Lives

The applications of remote viewing in your daily life are obvious, but it can also be applied in your professional world. Look into a company that interests you. Do this now. How does it function? Look around the various departments, take it backward and forward in time (backward works especially well because you can often verify this information). Go visit your favorite designer's studio or, better yet, the pitch meeting where your nemesis will present. Remember that attention is mobile and can go anywhere. If you make learning precognition interesting and pleasant, you will learn it more quickly. Once you master it, even just a tiny bit, you will find "viewing" totally irresistible when you have a free moment.

What distinguishes remote viewing from simple precognition or intuitive reading is that you can actually experience the totality of your target in its environment, in physical terms. If you get really good at this, people can feel your presence and you can feel theirs. This is called astral travel, astral projection, or remote viewing, once again an overmystified simple function of our energy. Try not to do this with your teenager (I am speaking to myself here), as it can be very intrusive and they will always know (intuit) on some level when you are doing it.

If you want to get your coworkers or employees doing some remote viewing with you without having them send you to a psychiatrist, try this approach: "I want to see what's going on here. You know what, let's just use our brains to have a look around. Let's really get in there. If we were there now, what would we be seeing? What would be going on? How would it be structured? Let's all get out of the box here and go wild. Extra credit for craziness. Just jump right in. Okay, where are you? Describe it."

Training Others in Remote Viewing

As with mediumship, remote viewing is fun to teach and fun to learn, especially in large groups. Here's a simple exercise: Write down a location that is familiar to you. It is very important that you know at the moment you do the exercise what the location looks like, who is in it, what its function is, and what its environment is like. You can tell the group in general terms where they are going or just tell them that they are going to the location that is written down on the piece of paper that you are holding.

Instruct your students to assume, when you tell them to begin, that they are at the location you have chosen. Tell them to use all of their senses to investigate their environment, to open drawers, to look outside, to smell, touch, and notice what interests them. Ask them to tell you what they are viewing at the location, including its use, where it is located in reference to its environment, and how they entered that place. It is helpful to allow their "thinking" senses to be focused on judging what they like and what they don't like about the target. I like to have everyone in the group jump in. I only tell people when I *don't* relate to the information they're giving me and never when I do. So, I remark on misses and not the hits. Ask people to give lots of impressions at once. Remind them that this is not a guessing game. What do their senses perceive about the target?

Here's another exercise: Have someone else put a secret object in a box. The best objects for this exercise have a clear form, color, history, and significance (I used a pink rose quartz heart on a talk show once, as I mentioned earlier). It is important that you do not know what is in the box, or the group might use telepathy to do this exercise. Tell them that when you say "begin," everything they experience with any of their senses will be a view of the target. It's good to ask them to draw a shape as well. When everyone is finished, open the box and pass the object around.

It is not uncommon in the beginning for a student to get a few correct qualities, and of course she will have some misses. Some students get their good hits at the beginning of the exercise, and then they start thinking; some have to get the noise out of the way initially and hit it at the end; others know what the object is before the exercise even starts and then get lost. Every person's process is different.

In a paired exercise the students can take turns viewing a location. Person 1 should give as little information as possible, such as simply identifying it as "Jim's house." Person 2, the remote viewer, should verbally report, and person 1 should take notes and give no response or feedback until the exercise is over. It is fun to move this exercise around in time. Have them view the target a year ago or a year from now. This is a good tool for evaluating actual property, like when you want to buy a home in an up-and-coming neighborhood and you ask your viewer to see the neighborhood five years from now. Remember to keep this exercise moving and make it fun. Serious, heavy focus does not help the process. Encourage your students, relatives, or colleagues to make mistakes, or they will never learn anything. Let them see you make mistakes as well. I do!

Beyond Remote Viewing

As with all of these abilities, try to check your impressions against fact. Try to buddy up with a friend and say, "I am going to visit you sometime in this hour; would you mind writing down when you 'feel' me or what shifted in your environment, or in your feelings at a particular time?" You can pick a time to describe where someone was at a particular moment and what was going on and ask them to verify it. All of these skills take practice, so . . . practice! Even with practice you will miss sometimes. I do, we all do. Perfection is an ideal, not a process.

This brings me to astral projection, or what happens when you bring more of your presence into a remote viewing location. The upside of astral projection is that you can actually make your presence felt in any given situation. The downside is that you tend to lose any intellectual or emotional perspective because you are now energetically part of what is taking place. So when would you want to use this skill?

Let us say that a loved one is at a distance and having a hard time. You wish you could be with her and lend support. You can use astral projection to bring your supportive presence to her. Whether or not she is consciously aware of it, she will experience your support. This differs from telepathic support in that your presence in astral projection is there in a more viscerally powerful, physical way. The students in my workshops tend to use one another regularly as intuitives and healers. They form lasting connections with one another, which we call our Circle. It is not unusual for a Circle member in crisis to report seeing a fellow Circle member at the exact moment that the person was sending healing. The sender also has the experience of having actually been with the target.

Often when a Circle member is in crisis, but not telling anyone about it, there will be a flurry of emails with feelings, questions, or observations about and to the person in need. Because my group has still not learned the skill of not emailing the whole list from their workshop (I say this with love, folks), I am copied on many of these cyclones of attention, so I get to observe them firsthand.

I have a very sloppy, very informal email newsletter that I send out to students when the spirit moves me. Often when I am going through a rough time or am ill, I will ask them to send remote healing and/or email readings. It is not unusual for me to "see" a few of the students around the house and then have them email me that they were working on me or had a detailed dream about me at the time. Once again, both the documented time and the accurate details confirm the experience.

My son has asked me many a time to not think about him when he is at school because he can feel me and it is distracting. He sends me text messages just as I am worrying about him (just as he is doing what worried me in the first place).

I am sure that many of you have had the experience of being totally focused on someone only later to find out that they were in need of you.

Whether you realize it or not, all of you have focused enough attention and energy on a loved one for long enough that he felt, heard, or even saw you. You have had an effect on him just as others have had an effect on you in this way. This can be an incredible gift, as well as a useful tool.

Here is another example: A meeting is happening that you want to have an effect on. You can make your presence felt by using this technique. I suggest that you experiment with both remote viewing and astral projection. You will likely find many uses for them in your own life and business that I have not thought of, and combined with some of the other intuitive skills in this book, you will have a dynamic process for influencing events.

I especially treasure the way astral projection can provide moments of peace during difficult times. I will often "visit" places of prayer or contemplation when I am having a particularly dispiriting day. When I have a disagreement, I will often view or visit what actually happened to see if perhaps I have drawn a faulty conclusion. These tools are meant for you to use easily, with fluidity, and productively in all areas of your life. They are ways to understand, influence, and connect to the world around you when you cannot physically be present; in fact, they are often more powerful than being physically present because of the subtlety they allow.

When you integrate remote viewing into your daily life, you will find that without having to do a remote viewing exercise you will recognize situations that you must walk into, and you will be comfortable and prepared when you do so. You will also have a greater sense of where the people in your life are, have been, and will be and be able to respond to them more appropriately. When people tell you stories, you will find your attention in the scene they are describing. In fact, in my workshops I often have to remind people to "stay in the room," since remote viewing and the accompanying astral projection are so automatic.

As with all intuitive work, it will be easier to view targets accurately that you have not seen and that you know very little about. The mind wants to reason, and you have to be experienced and well practiced to forget what you know, allowing intuition to give you a clear read.

It is good, between targets, to go back to your resting position of attention, which should be the best possible experience of being you in the present moment.

When you master remote viewing, you will be able to attend parties without dressing up and get all of the good gossip; you will be able to crash your competitors' meetings and plan your garden more effectively. You will be able to visit your child's classroom and see what is really going on, and even make your presence known when necessary.

Remote viewing is best done very quickly. In and out. Find what you are looking for and leave. The more mobile your various intuitive abilities are, the more useful they will be in your life. On the other hand, if you are using this to make your presence known, you may want to hang around awhile.

Refining Your Skills at Remote Viewing

Here are some exercises that you can use to develop this powerful intuitive skill. Feel free to modify them or add your own to meet your unique situation and needs.

Remote Viewing Process 1

Choose a location that you can verify.

- Am I looking for something specific? _____

_____

_____

_____

- Where do I choose to go today? _____
  _____
  _____

- I visited this target at the following time and observed the following activities, people, and environment: _____
  _____
  _____
  _____

- Write 1st time: _____
  _____
  _____
  _____

- Write 2nd time: _____
  _____
  _____
  _____

- Write 3rd time: _____
  _____
  _____
  _____

If you find this exercise too confusing, put it aside for now and return to it later. However, it is a fun exercise, as everyone gets different impressions and details about the location.

Remote Viewing Process 2

What future situations or locations do I want to view?

- Target: _____
  _____

- Responses: _____
  _____
  _____
  _____

- Verification (this of course will have to be done in the future): _____
  _____
  _____
  _____

- Target at a future date: _____
  _____

- Write observations: _____
  _____
  _____
  _____

What do I need to view again in my past to move forward in my life more effectively?

• Event: _____
_____

• Observations: _____
_____
_____
_____

• Effect on me: _____
_____
_____
_____

What do I see in my remote viewing that is distracting, upsetting, or unhealthy? I commit to shifting my attention to my embodiment when this happens (work on one thing at a time).

• Observations: _____
_____
_____
_____

Remote Viewing Process 3:
Remote Viewing for Transformation

Tell yourself: Today I am going to take a single challenge in my life (love, business, or anything else) and use remote viewing to show me a self-empowering perspective on it. I am going to allow intuition to choose the locations, and I am going to do this throughout the day, recording my data but not evaluating my data until evening.

- Challenge: _____
  _____
  _____

- Past location: _____
  _____
  _____

- Present location: _____
  _____
  _____

- Future location: _____
  _____
  _____

- When I review this data, this is what my remote viewing has accomplished for me today: _____
  _____
  _____
  _____

- Where do I visit when I need comfort, inspiration, or strength? _____
  _____
  _____

Remote Viewing Process 4:
Astral Projection

Pick a person or situation you want to be part of right now.

You may want to do this sitting or lying down and with your eyes closed, although it is not necessary to do it this way. However, this position will remove some of the distracting experiences from your environment. This exercise is most effectively done if you do the Quick Hit for remote viewing at the beginning of the chapter first, then deepen the experience using these steps.

View your target. As you view your target allow the experience of where your body is right now to become loose and blurry. Allow your senses and your attention to view your target in a way that you are part of the scene, part of the structure. Sense your interconnections to what and who are around you and your effect on the target, as well as its effect on you. Now you can move freely, interact, touch, talk, move things, anything you choose to do.

When you are done you may want to take notes on what has occurred and any shifts you sensed in the situation because of your presence. To finish, embody yourself in the here and now.

Using Remote Viewing during Sleep

Write down the targets you wish to visit and what you expect to find there. It is often helpful to choose one target, someplace or something whose structure or dynamic you need to evaluate in depth. Remember, if there is a real need or gain in doing an exercise, your subconscious will be more likely to allow intuition to prevail.

In the morning, the moment you wake up, notice where your attention is, what you remember from the night, how you feel, what is on your mind, whom you are thinking of, and so on. When you have documented all of your information, use your remote viewing to hop around your day and prepare you, as you brush, floss, and dress, to readily respond in the most powerful way.

The Location from the "Throwing You into the Deep End" Exercise on Page 162

Is there any chance you drew a tall obelisk-like form, something that seemed foreign, with lots of people? Perhaps you drew a stick or you saw a French flag, something that attracts tourists, something visited around the holidays, and so on. Did you think of a French film or a French friend? Did you get a sudden hankering for café au lait, escargot, or a croissant (I'm serious)? Did your attention go to something in your own environment that was tall and thin or French? If any of this happened, it is because I gave you the coordinates of the Eiffel Tower.

CHAPTER 7

Precognition

Your future depends upon many things, but mostly on you.

—FRANK TYGER

Quick Hit Exercise for Precognition

1. Ask yourself a question about the future. Write it down.

2. Go do something else—take a shower, start to prepare dinner, or read a magazine.

3. As you do that chosen "something else," every time a non sequitur to what you are doing hits you from left field, jot it down.

4. Keep doing something else as you jot down your impressions.

5. Sooner or later the answer to your initial question about the future will literally hit you over the head.

6. Check out its probability using traditional information. If this information is in conflict with your intuition about the future—as it often is—look at all of the left-field information you received while doing something else. It is likely that you have given yourself unrelated but accurate information about future events leading up to your answer. The schema goes something like this: if *a* happens and *b* happens, chances are often, but not always, that *c* will happen as well. If it is a real emergency, chances are your intuition will give you the answer without your asking. That's its job.

What You Experienced in the Quick Hit

Precognition uses the same mechanism as intuition, although to get a truly accurate answer you probably employed many of your intuitive skills, including telepathy, mediumship, remote viewing, as well as your sense of precognition. Precognition saturated your mind and senses, along with everything that you noticed in your environment (the picture you had never observed in the hallway of your lobby, an ad for your competitor's company, or a dark color when anyone mentioned the price of the yen). Unlike your perception of these skills in the present, your precognition probably gave you a sense of choice, some different courses of action or response as you were gathering information.

Raise Your Hand If
You'd Like to Know the Future

If you want to spend more time more effectively on your couch, precognition, or telling the future, is an essential skill. Other than the very helpful and correct answers to questions such as "Should I bring an umbrella today?" precognition helps you tidy up habits of making false starts, taking the wrong turns, and showing up unprepared. It crushes pipe dreams and replaces them with a real, achievable future, which often far surpasses your imagination. When you have an accurate sense, even an incomplete one, of what the future will bring, you can put the needed energy into finding resources in yourself, in your life, and in your choices to be right as often as possible.

I am going to give you many different ways to perceive the future. Many people say, "Oh, I don't want to know the future," which, I have to confess, is as alien to me as "I don't eat chocolate." However, I feel like I need to address those among you who are under the mistaken assumption that if you close your eyes when a baseball is headed toward you, it won't hit you. The reason to see the future is to be able to prepare for it and, when desirable, change it. Those of you who won't allow yourself to see the future often get hit by "bad luck" (no such thing, just bad preparation) over and over again in your relationships, investments, businesses, health, and so on. The excuses I hear for not wanting to see what lies ahead vary from the 1960s attitude of "I take it as it comes" to the neurotic 1990s sentiment of "I would be terrified." The reality is that you see the future whether you want to or not, and your subconscious is reacting to it all of the time. Maybe you are avoiding love to avoid loss, or sabotaging yourself somehow to avoid success because you know at some point you will be cheated in business, and so on. Unless you are aware of the fears that motivate you, you will be making faulty decisions based on a future that you know enough to react to, but are not conscious of enough to affect. The empowerment that comes from knowing that you *can* change what frightens, saddens, or displeases you is immense.

YOU CAN USE PRECOGNITION
IN COUNTLESS WAYS:

- To create changes in the present that will create the best possible future

- To forecast the stock market

- To define what is in your sphere of influence and what is not

- To predict the future of anything or anyone

- To direct your resources, attention, and energy where you have the influence to create change

. . . all from your couch.

As you are reading this you are predicting the future. In each moment, even in your sleep, you are living in many different "time zones." During certain moments you are probably well aware of experiencing aspects of your past, but the idea that you are experiencing your future may be so alien to you that you repress the experience, or, if anything, chalk it up to imagination. My students often report depression, anxiety, and other psychiatric symptoms that crop up long before a difficult future even manifests in their lives. When you redefine your reality to include the awareness of your past biases, you can live more fully in the moment and respond more effectively for your future. A well-balanced intuition gives you just enough sense of a future event so that you can act in your best interests in the present, often without knowing every detail of why. Intuition (in the form of precognition) can also alert you in time to act to avoid the event (like selling your tech stocks before the crash, even though everyone else believes they will keep going up, for example) or prepare for it (like getting a job even though your household seems fine and you have more than enough money).

However, I would like to mention here that I do not believe in training children in this type of intuition, as they are already far too intuitive for their own good and lack the intellect and ego function to differentiate between feeling and intuition. They also lack the experience to act responsibly on their precognition. A child's function, you see, is to observe what everyone else observes consciously and to use Socratic questioning and reasoning to learn about the world. However, noticing intuition will help them be proactive and empowered. We can teach our children to pay attention when something is off and to use both their own good sense and experience to find a trustworthy adult to aid them. In this way, intuition is engaged in an organic way (as with creativity) to help children be safer, more proactive, and empowered.

Oddly enough, the sixties generation's focus on going with a feeling is somewhat counterintuitive in that one often does not know what the feeling is about because the event hasn't happened yet. However, what precognition *can* do is lead you to identify what will likely happen as it guides you through a potential solution or outcome. Please be aware that I am not talking about dramatic, life-shattering actions here; most of your life-enhancing actions are quite subtle (because they meet needs that you do not yet have and address problems before they occur). Taking a class in writing, finding a new direction for your company, or learning how to administer an injection properly—whatever it is that you are guided by your intuition to do—will prepare you for what is to come, while also giving you a sense of accomplishment and pleasure. It is devastating to "know" that in ten years you will get a divorce and have a child to support on your own. It is, however, very efficient and empowering to prepare effectively for life's changes long before you are consciously aware of the need for preparation.

To recap, somewhere within you actually knows what lies ahead. As I explained previously, you may respond to it by doing seemingly irrational and ineffective things (such as avoiding success so that you are never robbed, instead of promoting your own achievement and self-protection in the appropriate ways) or frenetic, desperate things (as often happen when you are in a relationship that you know will end badly, perhaps to direct your attention away from the future). When you allow yourself to perceive the future, you empower yourself to participate fully in its creation.

You will find that in this chapter I will often use "subconscious" and "intuitive" together or interchangeably. Try to understand that intuitions that we are not willing or able to be aware of consciously are deeply stored in the subconscious. This is because there is much that would be too disorienting for us to see too clearly. We are also making choices every minute that affect the future. That is why it is sometimes easier to predict world events that you have no effect on than it is to predict when you will fall in love, which, believe it or not, is controlled by your choices. This is also the answer to the question "If we predict a future event, how do we know that we have not created the event?" By predicting things that lie beyond our sphere of control, be they personal or universal, we can see the power of prediction in action. By predicting things that are to some degree affected by us, we can see the power of our own energy to create change.

There is often a deep inner sense of "being on to something," however, the information is typically not clear enough for us to act upon it. You tend to allow in your conscious mind only the thoughts that you accept as real. The subconscious protects our perception of reality in this way. You do not have to believe that you can tell the future to be aware that you can; you do, however, have to suspend judgment just enough to allow yourself to document the precognitions you receive.

So how do you suspend judgment? For starters, follow my directions with discipline. Don't worry about the narrator in the back of your head telling you that this is ridiculous. Let the narrator speak, but do the exercises anyway. Rip the cover off the book if you have to and replace it with the cover of *How to Fix a Car.* One of the best ways to work past judgment is to write down or record the odd ideas and things you notice as you begin this chapter and then simply review them over time. What will happen is that you will see/hear that you somehow were able to predict events relating to your questions and concerns. This awareness, in turn, allows the subconscious to make you increasingly aware of this information without jarring your vision of reality. It requires practice, but you will see that it won't take much time for the process to make sense—if you are diligent about doing it. It is pretty straightforward: notice, record, review.

How many times have you ignored your feelings and ended up on the wrong track? A simple investigation of your attention to your senses might have kept you from making some avoidable mistakes. Now, not all of your difficult feelings are related to future events. So, how do you know the difference? Well, you start by asking yourself what reasonable, doable action would make you feel better. When I say, "Ask yourself," I do not mean that you should chew on the question for hours or days. Simply know that you want to resolve the feeling, and over time you will find that the actions you need to perform will come to you.

Remember the periphery, as precognition takes place at the periphery of focus, that nebulous domain where you may not be inclined to explore, thinking perhaps that it does not matter. It all matters—especially the periphery. You may say, "If intuition is telling me that my grandfather will die, how do I feel better about that?" You may decide to spend more time with him, you may finally tell him how grateful you are for his kindness or how angry you are for his violence, or you may simply come to terms with your relationship with him in advance so that when the loss occurs you are prepared. If it is an avoidable event, you may help him to avoid it.

Decades ago there was a mass shooting in the Rome airport. I often traveled to Rome, and I was frugal about how much I spent on airfare. I had been anxious for a few weeks before my trip, and at the last moment I decided, out of the blue, to cough up the extra money to change my discount ticket and paid the monetary penalty. I would have arrived at the Rome airport at the time of the shootings had I not done so. If I had literally "seen" the shootings I would have gotten so anxious that I wouldn't have been able to take action. Precognition did the smart thing for me and gave me the information and necessary course of action without making me so scared that I was unable to act.

Okay, So You've Seen the Future—Now What?

Precognition rarely tells you to take dramatic action that can suddenly disrupt your life or the lives of others. Very little in life or business requires such extremes, and your intuition "knows" so far ahead that it wouldn't unsettle you with drama by giving you an eleventh-hour warning—unless, of course, your subconscious wants that kind of drama. That is usually emotion speaking. When the actions require radical change (like when I sold all my son's tech stocks, which had done so well and seemed poised to do even better), usually they make sense and can be validated by other data (in this case, his tech fund had done very well, and even if I sold before it hit the top it was a win for him; there was a reasonable chance that the tech market would become vulnerable, and so on).

The future is not set in stone but is as fluid and susceptible to change as the present moment itself. Some things are within your field of control, and some are not. The movement of the commodities markets, for example, is not within your field of control, unless you are one of the major players. However, whether you bet that the market will go up or down is very much in your control. Part of the gift of precognition is the ability to position yourself to achieve the best outcome for *you*. When something is within your control (for example, you feel that the product your company produces will have a short life span in the marketplace), you can use your skills to find out the "why" and how to avoid the unfavorable outcome (in this case, a repositioning of it in the marketplace and the development of one of the company's other products). The beauty of precognition is that the same sense of intuition that warns you that something is amiss will also give you options to correct it.

How Does Precognition Work?

Although there are many different ideas about how precognition works, please allow me to give you mine and see if perhaps you can experience it as I do.

Right now imagine and experience, with all of your senses, the immediate present. What are you feeling? What is going on inside you, around you, in your environment, and in the universe as far as you care to extend your knowledge and perceptions? Stay in this moment. You may find that in this moment you can't help but know/experience many different things: how your partner or friend is feeling, what he or she is doing, something specific about the world, what you notice in the room, what you need to accomplish today—an entire array of events, experiences, and perspectives available in this single moment alone.

Now consider that in this same moment your past also exists. You are having a conversation with your third-grade teacher about an extension on a homework assignment and wishing you hadn't worn such an itchy sweater. You are aware that your mother is worried about what she will be making for dinner and that your teacher just lost her husband to cancer (even though you have no idea what cancer is at the age of nine, but regardless, the word somehow sticks in your mind).

Now also consider that in this same moment your future also exists. You are planting your balcony. The sea air feels cool and lovely against your skin. You are in the middle of a book you really enjoy but are not quite ready to go inside and continue reading.

The way to see it is this: in every moment you are experiencing the past, the present, and the future—from your own perspective and others' as well. It is as if all three "times" are simultaneously happening in a single place.

That said, as easily as you can change the present by making a phone call, changing your position on the couch, walking outside, or taking an aspirin, you can just as simply change the past or the future. Experiencing an existent future allows me to decide in the present what to change to affect that future. In my experience, everything is mobile and fluid, and the more you can create an experience of this mobility/fluidity, the more you can use it to create change. Although you need your senses of reality and judgment to function properly, they may also restrict what you can do with your energy, as they are self-imposed frameworks of limitation and energetic organization. What I mean by this is that you cannot simply command your mind to accept more convenient beliefs, but you can try doing little things that show you evidence, supporting new judgments that may allow access to new and more useful versions of reality. It is the experience of another truth that will change how you can use your precognitive ability.

As you read this, allow yourself to be as aware as possible of the details of this moment. What are you experiencing? What is around you? How do you feel? Where is your attention drawn? I know it may seem repetitive, but it is precisely this connectedness to the now that will help you to understand a broader, more complete sense of *your* now.

What parts of your past experiences, conversations, and feelings are darting in and out of your present experience of this moment? Allow yourself to be aware that the past always creeps into the now, existing in the present moment, and acknowledge that awareness, but bring your focus back to your consciousness of the present.

Now, observe how you are being drawn toward the future. Perhaps you experience this awareness of the future as worry, or hope, or keeping track of what you have to do. Don't worry about the details; instead, simply allow the awareness of the future and notice its detail. Every time your attention drifts to the future, notice it and bring your attention back to the present.

Working within your most probable belief system, you can only change time in what you call "the present." It is with present awareness being guided by information about the "future" and allowing us to reformulate the "past" that you can create miraculous change. Why do I use the word *miraculous*? If you are able to do, create, manifest, or achieve something that you never believed you could, you would call that a miracle, right? Something amazing, something outside the realm of possibility . . .

Welcome to the world of miracles.

Addressing the Skeptics

I know that many of you are skeptical about your ability (or perhaps anyone's ability) to predict the future. You may remember many times when you just knew something was going to go a certain way and—it didn't. I, too, remember times when I was clueless about something I should have been paying more attention to. One of my favorite self-thrashings is, "If you're so psychic, why didn't you avoid disaster, smarty?" There are explanations for these moments of misguidance and blindness (the subconscious is really *sub* conscious), but the reality is that most of your decisions, from the tiniest ones, like what to pack for lunch, to the more significant ones, like how to prepare for the future, are all actually part of your precognitive matrix. If you were to inspect a day, let alone a week, a month, or a year, you would find that you make hundreds of decisions, many of which you cannot base on experience or reason, and yet, somehow, you make those choices correctly. How can this be? Well, something else is at work here: you are responding to a pattern that you may not be consciously aware of, one that tells you what lies ahead. When you become more conscious of this predictive pattern, you can make better decisions about the future. In fact, you can create a better future, starting right now.

Science is interested in precognition as well. There have been many experiments done in the field of precognition, some even funded by the government. If you do a quick Internet search on science and precognition, you will find more evidence for precognition's existence than there is room for in this book. In one such experiment, believe it or not, subjects responded to a loud noise three to five seconds before the noise occurred.

Precognition Has Its Limits

Much like all human skills, precognition is performed by humans, and for that reason it is subject to interpretation and error. You will rarely get a complete picture. What you will get are pieces to assemble, and the more you practice the more accurately your completed puzzle will emerge. Let me give you an example of a mistake in precognition that I recently made. A friend of mine was fired from her job. She had not saved much money and was very worried about how she would pay her bills. She called me, and I "saw" her having more than enough money to meet her bills, so I figured that she would somehow or other get her job back. I figured wrong. Instead, her mother died and left her money. I was looking at the wrong target, or question, and there-fore I made an error. The question I was answering was, "Will she be able to pay her bills?" not "Will they rehire her?"

The most common precognition-related question I get is, "How will I know that I am really telling the future and not just wishing/dreading?" Although there are some signs that can subtly elucidate the answer to this question, the real answer is that you won't know. The more you practice, however, the more accurate you will become, which is something you can check if you docu-ment your readings and check them consistently at a future date. It also helps to allow as much information to come to you as possible and not to limit what you notice and document to what you think refers to your target/question.

There are many theories about how precognition works. One is that time is actually a place and not a continuum, so all events are happening now and already exist. Another is that events are energy dynamics or vibrations that can be followed forward, like a rolling bowling ball; the intuitive is viewing the ball's trajectory. There is the grid theory (best looked up online) and many others that I can't explain. I have my own opinion, which I will do you the favor of keeping to myself, since it is only an opinion. What I know from observations of thousands of people over thirty years is that we are all able to receive precognitive information and that the more we practice and document our future perceptions, the more useful, predictable, and reliable a skill it becomes.

So, the more you notice, document, and integrate the information you receive, the more complete is your map of the events leading up to your answer and the more clearly you will be able to verify the information.

In my thirty years as a practicing intuitive, I have found precognition to be reliable but not perfect. I am sure that you are looking for the perfect process, a way that can ensure you will never, ever make a mistake. It just doesn't exist. Precognition, however, is pretty dependable when you train it, but things can go wrong, and as with anything else, there are precautions you can and should take. One of the ways to protect yourself from the unreliability of precognition is to try to lead a life where precognition is a daily practice and try, with as much discipline as possible, to *write your future down*. In doing so, you will have data available when the events you predict do or do not occur, to indicate to yourself that you are on track or way off base. The more you take future-telling out of the arena of magic and allow it to serve you as a simple survival tool, the more accurate a tool will it become for you. Although mystifying things can make them more romantic and interesting, the truth is that the more steps you add to a dance, the harder it becomes to do it correctly. Telling the future should be a way to simplify your life.

Are Premonitions Precognitive?

Premonitions are usually warnings that something bad is going to happen, whereas **precognition** refers more generally to knowing positive as well as negative outcomes in advance. Genuine premonitions are real phenomena, and evolution has provided us with intuition (in its various forms) as a survival tool. After all, knowledge of impending dangers or disasters improves our chances for survival enormously.

Instead of getting paralyzed by the premonition, or submitting to a knee-jerk reaction, sit with the premonition. What is it telling you? Premonitions don't always present themselves in black-and-white. For example, you may get a sense of an imminent earthquake. That may be a warning of an actual earthquake. Or the earthquake may be the symbolism your subconscious mind is using to warn you about a massive upheaval in your life.

When you receive a premonition, ask yourself these four important questions:

1. What is going to happen?
2. When will it occur?
3. What do I want to happen?
4. What can I do to change the outcome if it's not what I want?

When you get a premonition, can you change the outcome? Yes, because if you couldn't affect the outcome, your subconscious wouldn't be bothering you with the warning. If we accept the notion that these types of intuitive tools are functions of evolution, well, there's no survival value in warning you about something that is inevitable, is there? The exception here is that, as with all intuitive skills, your subconscious can use your ability to predict and seek out your fixations and neuroses. For example, if you feel the world is unsafe, you may predict earthquakes that you can do nothing about, or epidemics that you have no control over. This is why it is so important to train your awareness and your life to be focused on the areas that empower *you*.

Premonitions can come to us in dreams or out of the blue. But we wish for things and worry about things all the time. So how can you tell whether a premonition is genuine? One way is that it will appear out of the blue, outside your normal wish-worry cycle. You can, however, train your intuition to be more alert. The key is to realize that everything you notice has meaning and that what you sense in your surroundings—especially what your attention focuses on—is *not* random. Premonitions confuse us because they are so very different from what is happening in the now. It's hard to tell whether we're responding in the moment to what's going on right now or to what we've just been warned is about to happen.

Should we heed premonitions? I say, if it doesn't cost us much to heed a strong premonition, then we probably should. At the very least, we should investigate the warning.

Guidelines for Doing
Precognitive Readings

First, a general outline:

- Know your question or target.

- Follow your attention and document your information.

- Do not try to evaluate your information as you receive it.

- Sometimes you get information without getting a complete answer, or even an answer at all. This often happens when there are variables that you have direct influence over. When this happens, know that the flashes of insight that seem to come from left field when you are finished "reading" are probably more pieces of information with which to answer your question.

Let's see what it's like to apply this to actual questions. For the sake of simplicity I am going to give the complete process for each step. When you want to know about a specific time or event in the future (Is my party going to be a success? Will I be healthy on my seventieth birthday? When will the price of oil be less than twenty dollars a barrel? What will the reaction be to this product when it is released on June 30?), there are a few ways to go about it:

Decide on your target and assume that your attention will go there. Remember, your target can be anything that you want your intuition to gather information about.

Don't direct your attention to it in any way. Document everything you notice (or, if giving a reading to someone else, vocalize everything you notice). Once again, much of it may not make sense to you or even seem to address your target. Keep reporting and you will find yourself with an understandable set of facts. The idea is to report until either you or your subject can piece together an answer. With practice you will find that you get your answers more directly and literally.

Allow your target to come to you and get a clear answer, yes or no. Then allow your attention to investigate the reason you got either "yes" or "no" and document/report. As you do this you will find that you visit different points in time with your attention. Sometimes your "yes" becomes a "no," and vice versa. Here's a simple example. For the question "Will I ever have a home of my own?" the answer might be "No, I don't see [hear, feel, smell] that I will have a home of my own." But as you follow the question forward in time, you may start to feel subtly that you *will* have a home to share with a partner, and the desire for your own home will feel more like a reality, and less like a desire. We all experience time differently, and part of learning to read into the future and placing things in time is to be aware of how you tell where you are in time during a reading.

Start in the present moment and follow your target toward the answer to the question. For example, you might ask, "When will be the best time to sell my house in the next five years?" You follow real estate prices forward to the highest price in the next five years. You will find that you will just naturally stop at the right point. To be sure, you can allow your attention to go forward after that for the full five years. Much of your peripheral information will explain why things happen, as well as give you the seemingly unrelated data leading up to your desired outcome that will show you that you are on the right track.

Maybe what you "see" aren't real estate prices at all. Maybe when you ask yourself this question, you see a piece of fruit looking particularly tasty, and then you drop it on an icy sidewalk and find that it is rotten inside. You may be one of those people who are not yet ready to present literal intuitive data to himself or herself. This means that you will instead have to interpret your symbols.

Of course, ultimately with practice you will go from clues to a more literal experience of the future. Some people start out literally and only receive metaphoric answers when the subject becomes too embarrassing or upsetting for them to intuit in plain old English.

Take Your Conscious Mind off the Ball—Your Subconscious Won't Forget It

Here's what I'd like you to do next: as you are reading this chapter, jot down all of the distractions that keep your attention from what I am saying. Every time you are distracted, write a word or two describing what is distracting you, and possibly why.

While you have been reading, what else have you been aware of? Where has your mind drifted? What have you been noticing in your environment? If these peripheral flashes in your awareness were information to answer the question I asked you to pose at the beginning of this chapter, how would the information instruct you? Ask yourself another future question now. Write it down and then let us speak a bit more about precognition.

Precognition, as with all intuitive skills, happens in the periphery of your attention. You pick your target or question and then you figuratively take your eyes off of it long enough for your conscious mind to move aside, to let intuition provide information from another source. Try looking at one word on this page for a full minute. Do this now.

As you do this, the word itself will become fuzzy. If you allow this to happen, information will form around you that will define what you are really looking at. Okay, notice what word you chose and quickly be aware of one or two thoughts that floated around you as the word became fuzzy. Now allow those few thoughts to tell you something about the significance of the word in your life right now. If there is no connection now, write the word and the thoughts down and return to it later. Chances are that your peripheral awareness will have given you some valuable information.

When using precognition, it is the same process: you choose your target, your "word," perhaps even jot it down, and then you allow yourself to be distracted by other thoughts or experiences. At a certain point you will be drawn to a particular awareness, and that awareness will lead you to another, and another, and your "reading" will begin.

The difference between creative visualization, brainstorming, and intuitive skills such as precognition is that in the case of precognition, you allow your awareness—what you see, feel, remember, taste, smell, and know—to lead you. You do not try to search for or create this information; you simply follow it. The first sensations may not make sense. You may ask yourself if your child will get into a certain college. The first things you may be aware of are the curtains in the room, or the red fringe on the table, or a show you put on when you were a child, or a feeling of nostalgia; and then the pieces come together and you realize that the curtain resembles a painting in a hall that you saw in a college brochure. You may feel sad that your child is away, laugh at how hard you worked to send him to the college of his choice, see him transferring during his second year to a place where he can ski, and so on. Remember that when you do a reading, you can check its veracity against itself later on, down the line. The *more* information you get, the *more* data you will have to prove your intuition right (or wrong).

For example, on an Irish radio show in early July 2008, they asked me to give their listeners a little intuitive "hit." At the time, the loudest voice in the market said that oil prices would continue to rise. I don't usually do parlor tricks by making such predictions on the air, but the host was so nice that I couldn't resist. So I simply noticed what was in my field of attention and said that I wouldn't be buying oil stocks for a while. The very next week, oil started a rapid and steady decline, plummeting by nearly two-thirds in price (as this book goes to press). I didn't search for what was going on in the market. I allowed something to come to me and, in the wonderful way intuition manifests, it addressed something in the market that anyone could relate to and follow.

Seven Golden Rules about
Using Precognition

There are times when you want the details of the future on demand. Especially in business, you often need to present rational data-based arguments to justify your actions. The rest of this chapter will give you some simple ways to tell the future and fill in enough of the details so that your intuition is based on logic, and logical to those around you.

1. The first rule of precognition is that you must work on empowering yourself to feel that you can create change. If you don't do this, you end up scaring yourself silly or lazing around, avoiding life, waiting for good things to happen. Neither helps you be powerful and proactive about your future. Sometimes change is just a matter of point of view. You need to *be* in a different part of the scenario instead of trying to change the scenario itself.

True, there are some things in the future you cannot change. In my previous book *Practical Intuition for Success,* I spoke about your sphere of influence and what lies outside it. Much more than you think is actually within your sphere of influence (see the chapter on creating new outcomes), but you may have to do the hard work to change your position in the event in order to bring your influence to bear. For example, you may experience that your husband will have or is having an affair. When you allow yourself to get more information on the event, you may be struck by his deep depression and sense of hopelessness. In looking for existing data, such as speaking to his cousin about the family, you may find that there is a history of depression in the family going back generations that they just weren't savvy enough to know was depression at the time (remember, whenever possible get nonintuitive supporting data). You may be able to change the event by guiding your husband to practices, doctors, or behaviors that address his depression and avoid the devastating self-treatment—the affair that he was moving toward. This may sound controlling, but I prefer to call it "aware." When you live life in a state of awareness, very few crises occur. Let's take this same scenario and postulate that your husband refuses to follow any course of treatment. This gives you a lot of time to fortify your life in a way that will allow you to leave, calmly address the event when it happens, speak with him about your awareness, or make countless other choices that will lead you to safety and joy. Sometimes the awareness on the part of one partner of a future event is all it takes to avoid the event altogether (see chapter 4).

2. *The second rule of precognition is to know what your questions are.* You need to know what the "what" is. When you know at least some of your questions or points of interest, you will know where to file the information when it comes in. Precognition does not always happen on demand. Have you ever forgotten a name and tried really hard to remember it without success? Hours later, in the shower, when you are thinking about which shampoo to use, the name pops into your consciousness. Such is the way with intuition. As you practice, the time between your being aware of the question and the answer will shorten so as to be almost imperceptible, but the process remains the same. Once you have the question, intuition needs time, without your focus on it, to travel around, gather data, and make a conclusion. I suggest writing your questions down, both the long-term and short-term ones,

especially for the ones that come up during the day. When I do a reading, I often simply jot down a word or scribble something down that represents the question for me. By the end of the reading I have a collection of unintelligible scribbles, which are, in fact, the miraculous little seeds of my answers.

3. The third rule is to give your focus a rest. Your intuitive attention needs time to travel and assemble information from various points in time and points of view. You cannot follow this process cognitively without getting confused, although you will get bits and pieces of it floating up into your consciousness. When you know your question, do something else with your attention. Often, during a reading where I have to get an answer fast, I take a sip of tea, draw some kind of doodle, stir my sauce on the stove, or try to talk about something else. Bottom line: distract, distract, distract!

4. The fourth rule is not to get wedded to your answer. As you deepen your awareness of the information you receive, your original conclusion may start to change. If you do not allow for this type of fluidity, you risk inaccuracy. Sometimes I will even call a client back when a piece of information comes to me that somehow alters the original conclusion I worked out with her.

Information that conflicts with your original hit may even come days later. Leave yourself open to integrate new data and change direction if necessary. It is the plasticity of intuition that makes it so accurate, and your data is constantly building on itself. Rarely will consciously generated intuitive data present itself in an "emergency, act now" fashion. Remember, your intuition is geared to forecast in a way that eleventh-hour warnings become rare as you integrate precognition into your decision-making process.

The other mistake that often happens with precognition is that you have chosen the wrong target or asked the wrong question, which becomes clear over time as you gather your intuitive information. "Is he cheating?" may become "Do I want to leave this relationship?" Perhaps he is cheating, but before putting all of your focus into that answer, you may be led to the fact that this relationship is no longer what you want, and your precognition needs to show you potential opportunities coming up for you that will encourage you to make a move at this propitious time (which, in the end, means he probably *is* cheating, or will likely cheat). With financial and world affairs you may wonder what the market will do, or if *x* will go to war with *y*, and all of your energy will be distracted there, whereas your real question may be, "What should I do now to benefit from these current conditions?"

5. *The fifth rule is to always be aware (and report to your subject if you are doing a reading for someone else) of what you "know" from outside information as distinct from what you intuit.* This will help both you and your subject know what, other than intuition, may be influencing your intuitive data. For example, I always let my clients know when I remembered something instead of getting the information from intuition. I find that my intuition is usually on target, especially if I follow the first four rules, but what I remember and know can sometimes lead me to bend my intuition to fit the "facts." Many mistakes are made in this manner, so it is best to be aware of what you "know" as you practice intuiting.

6. *The sixth rule of precognition is to let your awareness lead you even when it doesn't make sense or when you don't know where it is taking you.* Follow, follow, follow. Many of us are well trained in

creative visualization and brainstorming. Well, intuition is neither of those things. You are not creating anything or sourcing your subconscious for stored ideas. You are following a pattern of energy that knows where it will end up long before you do. You are being led, not leading. If you try to reason and edit as you do this work, you are being counterintuitive. If everything you perceive makes sense to you, then you are performing something other than precognition.

Often, your first intuitive sense of a question is not what you are looking for. This is where imagination and creativity push to take over the process. However, if you expect this reaction you will allow yourself to continue on intuition's journey, gathering data to create a result that is beneficial to you, even when all of the data is not.

My favorite relationship example of this was a woman whose question was about when she would have true love in her life. Her intuition (and other people's intuition in the group) led her to find out that her current partner, with whom she was not very happy at the time, was having an affair. She didn't believe the information until, over the course of the weekend, it led her to the evidence. To make a long story short, the affair was a catalyst for the partners to work on the relationship, and now, almost a decade later, they are very happy together and very much in love.

This was not the information she was looking for. She was instead hoping for some data on her timetable for a new love. Your judgment, fears, and hopes can lead you to ignore such vital information, but in time you unlearn this. It is also very helpful to do precognitive work in a group, as other people will not be as careful to ignore what you don't accept. Train your colleagues, your friends, and your family or start a group of people who are happy to exchange readings on a regular basis.

Last but not least, know that you can be wrong. When you are, do not beat yourself up, but instead evaluate where you made your mistake. If you find yourself making errors, you will likely ask yourself, "Where am I getting this information?" "How do I know it is intuitive information and not just me, thinking or remembering what I know?" When you are doing a reading, much of what you are getting are thoughts and ideas about things other than your target, maybe even some telepathy about what other people may be thinking about the situation. This is why it is important to follow all of the steps and pay attention, most of all, to the flashes that come in from left field. Follow your attention and report it, and at a certain point you will be forcefully drawn to sudden revelations about the true topic of interest at hand.

7. *The seventh rule is that when you lose your perspective, you lose your accuracy.* If you are panicked, furious, despairing, or hiding the truth from yourself about a particular issue, you cannot maintain enough distance from or perspective on your question to experience the clarity of intuition. During a recent economic crisis I put my investment money somewhere I didn't have to think about it, even though it meant losing prospective gains. Why did I do this? If I had a personal investment in the direction the market went, I would be unable to predict dispassionately for my clients. My most rational move was to stay clear and neutral, and to do that I needed to remove myself from my personal investments.

When love is not working in my life, I need to find a channel, a thruway in myself, where I can be detached from my personal experience. This might mean talking things out with a friend or therapist, writing letters to myself to get it out of me, doing something so pleasant that negative judgments are tempered or modified. However, what you need and what I need in these situations are different. It varies according to how you respond to disappointment and crisis and what soothes and pacifies you. Finding a clear internal channel for your information does not have to take years or even hours. You can build a repertoire of quick fixes to allow you to shift your state of being so that you can proceed with the task at hand, which is to receive accurate information intuitively.

Perspective, perseverance, and porosity (I do like alliteration) are essential if you are to be an accurate, precognitive intuitive. *Perspective* is the state of knowing where you personally stand on a question or issue. It is essential to know how you respond "under the gun"; you need a practice where you can find clarity within you when you are in crisis-response style. In order to be a great intuitive you need to be an aware human being, which, of course, requires a process.

When doing precognition or any other intuitive reading, you must *persevere,* which means you must be willing to work for clarity. The information your intuition provides and your subconscious allows will come in bits and pieces that you must weave together to understand, and then you must verify it all against what your logic and knowledge tell you.

Finally, you'll need to be *porous* enough in order to let the information flow in, but you must simultaneously maintain your sense of self. When you are doing intuitive work and opening up your perceptive boundaries, it is a given that you will be invaded by the strongest feelings, sentiments, opinions, and movements of action and energy around you. It is your sensitivity and porosity that allows you to perceive the information you need. As with most things, this gift has a double edge. You need to work to stay grounded and emotionally healthy and to not read what you *hope*, but what really *is*—your target, viewed with accuracy, not compassion. This is essentially the art of seeing reality as it is, and not as you would like it to be. As you become more open to the information, you may feel bombarded by the amount of data, feelings, precognitions, and other impressions you receive. This can really unbalance you. Those of you with good boundaries and focus will feel more grounded than those of you who are habitually all over the place. Knowing how you react to upsets will help you focus on finding your own center during those upsets, so that you can have the solidity to interpret your intuitive information accurately.

Using Precognition in Your Daily Life

Often in daily life you will simply want to know in general what is coming up for you. To begin the process of daily precognition, simply follow the feeling that stands out for you in that moment or day. Notice when your attention drifts and notice where it drifts.

For example, you wake up feeling happy for no particular reason. You follow this vague happiness and then have a sense that you will meet someone who will be special in your life. You make a mental note to wear something nice.

Or maybe all the details of a business deal look great, yet every time you think about it something annoys you. Instead of avoiding the issue of what may be wrong with the deal, you begin to ask yourself what more you should investigate before you close. Perhaps you get a sense that someone is being dishonest with you. When you become intuitively aware, great deals aside, you become alerted to other areas of contention that you will be able to confirm with facts down the line. It helps you review the deal in all of its details, eyes open and focused forward.

In your day-to-day practice, you can also just allow your attention, all of your senses, to wander around your life, forward into time. How do you do that? Start with the basics: practice, document, and verify. But how do you instruct your senses to look forward? Well, ask yourself, put your attention on the question of what is coming up for you, and notice where your attention is drawn.

As always with intuition, allow your senses to lead you even if you find yourself jumping around to unrelated ideas or not understanding the information you receive. Your intuition will follow its own tail to the head, and if you go with it you will find that you end up with a complete circle of information that is not only accurate, but also very much actionable.

Training Others in Precognition

A fun exercise for formal students of intuition, or even during parties, is what I love to call "the hit-and-run reading." For this you will need a package of identical index cards and a timer.

Someone needs to always reset the timer so that each person has exactly one minute to "read." Instruct each person to think of an important question he or she has about the future, and when the person has it, to write it on the index card. The question can be as specific or as general as the participant wishes. As a rule, the more specific the question, the more specific the answer it will generate intuitively.

The objective for each person in the group is to get many readings about his or her question. I suggest that this be done as a moving exercise so that there is less opportunity to get into the empathic state, where you read cues from the other person sitting across from you, as opposed to gathering intuitive data, as you normally would making the rounds at a party.

It is good to have a bell or gong to signal to people when to change positions (readers become the clients) and when to change partners. Do not open the cards. Intuition will direct your attention to the correct target information. The idea is that in the time allowed, as many people in the room as possible exchange readings with one another.

Ask each person to begin walking around the room, card in hand, until the bell rings. When the bell rings, everyone should exchange their card with a partner. The person with the brightest colored shirt (or the tallest person, or the person with the most jewelry, etc.) should be the "reader" first. When the bell rings again, the reader should simply report where his or her attention goes—in as conversational and as clear a way as possible (as if making a map for the client) and without stopping (so the mind doesn't have time to imagine, create, or reason). The reader should allow the attention to go to the answer of the other person's question.

This answer may be in many places and may be revealed in bits and pieces. Tell the partners not to look at each other as they do this, as feedback can mislead intuition. Tell the readers not to worry about or focus on what the questions might be. They must avoid their learned desire to reason and, instead, allow their intuition to lead.

They should follow their attention and report what they perceive even if it doesn't make sense to them. Ask them to be courageous about giving detailed reports of the impressions they receive. Remind them that things that don't make sense to them now are often the most accurate pieces of intuitive and precognitive data. The purpose of this exercise is not to be right but to give valuable, actionable information in a supportive way to a person who needs it.

Remind them also that neither do they have to reveal what their question is at the end nor should they ask what their partner's question was. (It might be personal.) Remind them that if their objective is to be "right," their attention cannot be on the target or be mobile enough to travel where it needs to go. They need to let go of "right" and allow their attention and senses to perceive.

It is helpful for everybody to have a little book to write down the information received from readers to compare the different readings (on the same target) later. I suggest this because memory is a tricky thing. It is much more efficient to write things down. Alternatively, when you are giving a reading, the information will be all about the other person, so there will be no need for you to remember it; in fact, it would only be mental clutter if you did.

Have the first person read for a minute, and then ring the bell and tell the second person to now do a reading on the partner who just read them (based on the unseen question on the card).

When each partner has had their minute to read, have everyone take their own card back and ring the bell so that they can find other partners.

Do enough turns to have each person in the room read everyone at least one time. The more tired you become, the less you will reason and judge your intuitions away. As a rule, your first readings will not flow as easily as when you really start to get into the pace of it. Think of it as cardiovascular exercise: the calories only really start to burn off when you've brought your heart rate up to a certain level—which takes time, diligence, stamina, and motivation.

The one-minute timer adds that extra level of excitement to the exercise. Each intuitive has only a minute to give his or her reading, and then everyone switches roles or partners. It raises the stakes and forces people to push past their limitations.

Remember, you can all be wrong, and everyone knows, on some level, aspects of their own information, so have fun with this and allow yourself to uncover a useful, enjoyable, and even social skill.

Improving Your Skill with a Daily Process

Here are six questions you can ask yourself on a daily or weekly basis:

- What questions do I need answered right now?

- Why are these questions important to me?

- What do I think the answers to these questions are?

- What do I hope the answer to these questions will be?

- What do I fear the answers to these questions are?

- What do I think I can do now to create the outcomes that I want?

Now, over the next few days notice the bits and pieces of information that come up, not just intuitively but in the world, the news, conversations with other people, and especially the ideas and thoughts that come in from left field, and jot them down next to your questions as you perceive they might apply.

Rewrite your top questions below. As you hear people speculate about future events during the day, observe the flashes of your intuition that tell you what is going to happen. Once again it is helpful to write it all down. As time passes, check your intuitive hits against reality. You will notice that the more you engage in this process, the more accurate you will become at predicting events.

Pick some things to predict from other people's conversations during the day that aren't important or charged for you. You will find that the more detached you are (or the more you can cultivate a detached state when you are attached to the outcome), the more accurately you can predict the future without the interference from your feelings, history, or judgment.

You may worry about the future as you go to sleep or fantasize about desirable outcomes. If you are like most people, you do a combination of both. Even distracting yourself from thinking about a question or problem is a subconscious focus on the question. There is really no effective way to trick yourself.

Precognition While You Sleep

As you prepare for sleep and loosen your attention to conscious thought, the events of the day, your reactions, your feelings, and your judgments, you are poised to allow true, pure, accurate intuition to assemble its guidance, which all happens as you sleep. I purposely do not call your sleep reasoning state your "dream state," as they are not the same. Many of your perceptions may actually take place when you are in a lower brain-wave state than REM dreaming. The nightly task of your dream state is to do psychological repair and assimilation, based on the intuitive work you do earlier. In this state you create new patterns, intentions, and desires based on having all of the information.

Answers have many pieces and reality has many perspectives. Putting all of this information together to give you the guidance that you need is confusing when you are thinking and reacting during the waking day, but the night is made for just these kinds of mysteries and puzzles. As your perceptions are freed and as your body opens, heals, and melts into the physical ease of sleep, you are finding the pieces of data you need to create strong, successful decisions, and each piece of the puzzle is effortlessly finding its natural place in an accurate representation of the future. What you need to do is to respond to it successfully. In your sleep state your subconscious, intellect, judgment, and feeling still function, but they do so in a more detached manner. In this state, equitable intuition reigns and is able to create the best total outcome for you. Answers are rarely without conflict, but even the conflicting data that you receive will be successfully negotiated by your sleeping awareness.

In the waking state, intuition occurs at the periphery, the sidelines of your awareness. In sleep, intuition *is* your full awareness. You already know your questions, your concerns, and the future that you hope to build. Your intuition is already working on clarifying the actions you can take and the changes you can make to create these realities in your life. You can help this process now by choosing a single statement that focuses your intuition on a single task for the night. You may want to put this book down for a moment as you allow that single statement to come to you. You don't have to make such an effort. You already know. You simply need to allow the awareness of this knowing to come to you.

When you have your night task or question, I suggest that you write it down. Keep a notebook or something to record your voice near your bed. When you awaken in the morning you will want to record the perceptions, feelings, ideas, concerns, and solutions that float into your consciousness immediately upon awakening. Much of this will not appear to address your question directly. Record it anyway. Add to it during the day from your "out of the blue awareness," where your attention is continually drawn while performing your daily tasks. What seems to slip in over and over again at the periphery of your awareness? With precognition, once you know your goals and you are managing your crisis reactions, intuition will take over and draw you, again and again, to the information that you need to make a correct decision for the future.

CHAPTER 8

Healing

Medicine can only cure curable disease, and then not always.

—ANCIENT CHINESE PROVERB

NOTES

Quick Hit Exercise for Healing

1. Decide whom or what you want to heal and the length of time you will engage in focused healing. You will find that the healing state is so healing for you that time will pass and you will begin to merge with your target (and therefore cease to have an effect on it), so it's key to keep your healings within a time framework. It also helps you internally organize how you will manage your energy and attention during each part of the healing.

2. Take a deep breath and bring in energy. You can do this in your mind's eye or literally hold it between your hands.

3. Allow your attention to go toward where or what you want in order to heal yourself, your life, or someone else.

4. Allow intuition to give you a representation of what is located there. Use your attention and breath to create a change. Allow your intuition to perceive this change as it occurs. This will be a quickly changing detailed set of observations, some of which will seem unrelated and surprising.

5. You will know instinctively and intuitively how to focus and what to do. Simply follow your awareness.

6. When the time is up, embody your healed self and reorient yourself in your body in the here and now.

What You Experienced in the Quick Hit

You picked a target and then you organized your own energy in the best possible way to heal your target (which, in turn, leads to your healing as well). Whether you felt the energy or not, I wanted to get you into the habit of focusing your energy and attention and being the leader in any energetic dynamic. That energy alone can help you transform and heal. However, many of you were also able to experience internal and external information about your target, in relation to its environment. Experience is always changing, as is energy, but we are trained in school to keep our attention focused and immobile. The practice of allowing your attention to move to where you need information, as well as the experience of using focus to create continuous transformation, is what healing is about.

When you returned to your embodiment of you, did you notice a different sense of yourself? Even if you were not your own target, the sending of energy (healing) and the reading of energy (intuition) are important energetic skills. Even when you are not doing intuitive work, your ability to read signals in your body and environment, and simultaneously be engaged and active, is a healing state of being.

Write down the target you picked if you have not done so already, and notice any changes in your target and its fortunes, now and in the coming days and weeks, that you may have catalyzed or predicted.

What Is Healing?

Simply stated, healing is directing energy to change something into a desired state of being. If you have fried an egg or made an ice cube, intervened in an argument or used a good idea to turn your company around, taken an action that made your stock portfolio strong or simply made a meal that was loved by your family, you have changed energy and performed a healing.

What is energy? Everything is composed of energy: your chair, your body, your environment, and your life—everything is made up of energy, which, in turn, has patterns that can be changed with intervention. That is what healing is all about, and it helps to think of healing as having two key components: *energy* and *attention,* which together constitute *action.* You will be using energy and attention alone to change energy, or change a situation, but as you do, I am sure that both intellect and intuition will provide the information and focus to take other kinds of action that may be needed as well.

YOU CAN USE HEALING IN COUNTLESS WAYS:

• To heal yourself or others, or even things or situations

• To lose weight

- To change a life, business, prosperity, or love pattern so that something new can occur

- To resolve conflict in relationships

- To create positive outcomes from chaos

- To rejuvenate the body

- To improve your own or someone else's mood

- To restart your car's stalled engine

- To influence the direction and outcome of any pattern of energy, event, or relationship

- To bring any system to a more functional, successful state of being

- To integrate disharmonious elements of a body, life, relationship, or company

- To throw a better party

- To strengthen a company

- To create and maintain healthy relationships

- To reclaim lost parts of yourself

- To provide care, help, and solace at a distance

. . . and many other functions that you will
discover on your own.

Let's backtrack for a moment. Everything, whether it is a company, a family, the pattern of your love life, or your physical reality, is energy. *Everything is energy.* This is not pseudoscience—it is science.

People often refer to "good energy" and "bad energy," and I am here to tell you there is no such thing. After all, can you actually qualify the energy that turns on a lightbulb? Good energy or bad energy? Energy is simply energy, until it is patterned or directed to take form or action. It is what you do with energy that makes the difference.

I am opposed to the idea that an illness in the body, such as the formation of a cyst or weight gain, is bad energy that has to be destroyed. What I do maintain is that all maladies are just energy in need of redirection. The most optimal healing position you can take is to love, to hear, and to use all of the various parts of you for your own well-being. Perhaps your excess poundage needs to be transformed into the energy to find your true love or to write the perfect novel. Perhaps a cyst needs to be transformed into your ability to set boundaries for the people in your life who bring too much poison into it. Perhaps your kidney stone needs to be transformed into your ability to ask for and receive the support from your family that gives you enough rest. Your back pain may be your need to be aware that your parents burdened you; in order not to feel badly about them or re-create the same situation in your life, you hold that pain, safe and sound, in your back.

People often confuse the intuitive healing state with creative or positive visualization, which we talked about earlier. They are very different. When you are in an intuitive state you are not creative or searching, or insisting on details. You instead allow the details to come to you, and as they do you integrate them into whatever you are doing. Often your intuition can give you a more complete healing than you could ever visualize, as you may have never experienced this state of well-being, love, success, health, or happiness before. It simply may not be something that you can imagine.

How Does Healing Work?

I wish I had a definitive answer to throw your way, but instead, here's a concept I'd like you to entertain. You don't have to believe it, you simply have to entertain it, play with it, and try it out. Think of the world, the whole world, your life, your past, present, and future, your family, your friends, your lover, your work, everything in your world as part and parcel of one giant organism. Your body is also part of this organism. Your body creates your world and the world you live in creates your body. Healing includes your multilayered experiences and abilities in the world; defining healing and its opportunities for and its effect upon *you*. When you change your body, you change your world. When you change your world, you change your body. Now, do everything in your awareness to experience your body as energy.

At any given moment each of us lives in a different world. As adults we choose much of the world we live in, and the more conscious and aware we are the more this becomes true. We choose how we experience this world, and because life is a circle, our experience then chooses the world we draw, created by our experience of it, and its effect on us. The more consciously we do this, the more effectively we live in the world we want, and the more efficiently we can use this energy to change our bodies, which, in turn, has a powerful effect on the world we inhabit.

Are you still experiencing your body as energy? Use all of your senses to experience your body as atoms of energy. See the atoms, moving and changing, feel them gathering new information and integrating it into their movement, smell the renewal of drive and dreams, taste the freshness of potential change, hear the dynamic alteration of their previously set patterns and content, and *know* that you have the power to create any change. It is your life, your body, your thoughts, and your history, but it is also only energy—simple, dynamic energy. As you read, continue to experience yourself as atoms of energy.

There is a story that I will remember forever. Many years ago there was a six-year-old girl who had contracted hepatitis from having her ears pierced in a shopping mall by nonsterile equipment that had been used on someone else. She was dying in a New York hospital from liver failure. She needed a new liver, but finding a small liver on short notice is not so easy. Her family was very Catholic, and the local priest who had been praying with them in the hospital room called me in to do a healing. I went to the hospital room with stickers and little gifts and when I had the girl's confidence I did a laying on of hands, which, by the way, everyone can do (more on this in a moment). After the healing, which I simply told the girl was my way of praying that she would feel better (it is important to use a language that your own self/body or subject can accept), I said my good-byes and left the room.

Her doctor grabbed me by the arm and practically dragged

me to the physicians' lounge, where he locked the door and began to berate me for giving the family a far-fetched illusion. "This child is going to die," he said, "and you are giving them false hope," as if the family, her parents, and her friends weren't already hoping that she would heal. At that age, behind a locked door with an enraged authority figure, I was so afraid of what else he might do to me that I was speechless.

Still, I came back the next day to see the girl as I had promised her family. The room was empty and I was afraid she had died. I asked the nurse, and she told me that the girl had a miraculous healing during the night and her liver function had returned to normal. She had been transferred to another floor. I was walking to her room when I saw the doctor who had accosted me the day before. He came toward me and snarled, "How do you know you caused the turnaround?" I never have good comebacks normally, but this time I replied, "Why do you care, isn't the patient well now?"

As for yourself, don't worry about how you heal or what you need to heal; just focus on getting all of the intuitive information in order to begin the process. Your pain is important, whether it is psychological, physical, or circumstantial. Your well-being is essential. Suspend all traditional ideas and the judgments that you have about healing in a certain way, and allow intuition to guide you toward all the help that you need to heal. Be your own best physician, which begins by being your own best friend.

Whether Healing a Person, a Company, or a Situation—Know Your Target

You can use the same techniques you would use to heal a body to shift the dynamic of your business, your wealth, your love life, or any other "body" in your life. We will use the human body as a metaphor and a training ground for all of the complex systems in your life where you can direct this ability to heal.

In order for a body to heal, many things need to be addressed. To start, you need to work with the patterns, history, beliefs, interactions, responses, messages, and the environment that created the dysfunction and continues to sustain it now. Any system, from a car engine to a multinational corporation to a person, has a history, trauma, a subconscious (or hidden mechanism by which it functions). Everything is some kind of "body," a dynamic system surviving within another dynamic system. That is why techniques that address physical healing can be directed to heal any "body." A business, too, has a history, its own trauma, a subconscious, and everything else that a person has, and so does any other situation or entity you can imagine.

Often when you do a healing, on yourself or someone else, your attention will be drawn to an incident or injury in the past that needs healing. Although you can heal the injury in the present, you can also heal it in the past. When you are performing healing on yourself or another, you need to access the most powerful starting point, the one that will have the most universal impact on the dynamic. That point is different for every person on every issue. Here is where you need to allow your senses and your intuition, the extension of your senses, to pull you toward the right first step. For weight loss, your first step in healing may not be physical. It may be emotional or located in a pain center of your body. It may be located in memory or in taste or a habit that has its root in something else. You may first need to address isolation or clothing choices or reading material. My point is that answers can and often will surprise you. As I said, every issue is different, and every person is different on every issue. One of the hardest things to do when learning to perform an effective healing is to trust some of the strange, counterlogical places our perceptions are led to in order to catalyze the change. Think about it: usually when you or someone else has a problem, you turn to all of the standard treatments, cures, and explanations, and more often than not those things don't work. I invite you to consider a new realm of solutions.

Throwing You into the Deep End, Once Again

An actual healing is more unified than these separate steps would suggest, but here they are:

1. Decide whom or what you want to heal.

2. Embody, and then fill your body and your embodiment with energy.

3. Hold your hands one foot apart, palms facing each other. Use your senses to "place" your target between your hands.

4. Allow the energy you are taking in as you inhale to flow between your hands and into the target.

5. Allow intuition to give you a representation of what is located there.

6. Use your attention and breath to create a change. You will instinctively know how to focus and what to do. Simply follow your awareness. You may experience yourself sending colors, heat, or cold, making elements of your target speed up or slow down, and alternating between different sending senses. You may move your palms to move the energy of your target.

7. Allow yourself to perceive the changes in your target as they occur. These will be a rapidly changing set of detailed observations, some of which will seem unrelated and surprising, which take place at the periphery of your attention.

8. Keep your attention focused on directing your energy and breath to the target between your hands.

9. When you lose focus, return to a resting state by embodying you.

Performing a healing is simple, but it takes practice to do it well. Again, I really suggest that you document your healing goals and their results. This will nudge your subconscious to use its own power resources and intuition to employ energy healing in your every action and in every area of your life.

Quickly, right now, rub your hands together as you breathe deeply. Use your inhalation to really puff up your body with energy and use your exhalation to release any thoughts and kinks in your muscles, neck, and jaw. As you read this, allow your thoughts and judgments to get lost in your vigorous breath. I know this is a bit of a gymnastics act while reading, but I am sure that you have engaged in worse contortions to accommodate your life. Breathe and rub your palms together. Now put your hands anywhere on your body and continue to be aware of your breath, providing energy to your hands. You can laugh while you are doing this or think judgmental thoughts, you can even go over your grocery list, as long as you are breathing and allowing the energy from the breath to flow out of your hands and into your body, whether or not you believe it is really working or happening. Congratulations: you have just done your first rough draft of a healing. Let's go a little deeper now.

Take a deep, active breath and generate the same energy with your attention and breath without using your hands this time (which, depending on the situation, can make you look a bit odd). Take a powerful inhalation and in your mind's eye find your target. No hands: just your attention and your breath.

Allow your intuition to provide you with a real physical sense of the target. Don't judge how you are representing your target— or, if you are one of those people who must judge, allow the target to be represented by your judgment.

Now, experience (by seeing, feeling, hearing, tasting, or just knowing) the target changing in the way you want it to, healing, and focus your attention and breath on its resolution, even if you do not have a clear sense of what the resolution or healing is. The experience of this will be unique to you. Everyone experiences it differently. Notice what is changing and continue the process.

As you do this you will notice that feelings, memories, messages, words, phrases, and judgments (just to name a few things) begin to come up to your awareness. Your body is not just flesh and blood, bone and organs, systems and glands. Your body is composed of your experiences, patterns, judgments, injuries, and self-injuries as well. Your body is composed of the projections of others that you have carried with you throughout your life, including those you received chemically in utero, your external life and its structures and all the people in it and the energy they generate. Your body is a complex physical organism, and its profound ability to change lies in all of these other patterns that your energy follows—patterns that can actually change. Awareness is the key to this change.

Positive results don't always feel good initially. Of course, in the unlikely event that you feel really ill as you do the healing exercise, you should certainly call your doctor, but what I am speaking of is the awareness of a series of discomforts that you have carried with you without being aware of them. You have dragged them along, repressing the pain they caused you, so that you could do all that you had to do every day. This lack of awareness has also blocked the awareness of your unique and individual cures, beauty, ability, and power to attract what you need—the very things that could make you comfortable and proud to inhabit the body you are in and change it in the ways you need it to change.

Are you still experiencing your body as energy? This is your reminder. To use the rest of this chapter effectively, this mantra should always be your starting point. It reminds you of the reality that your body is not a solid, unchanging mass, but instead a dynamic, living, ever-changing organism.

Body communication goes two ways. Your body and its memory, injuries, and functions communicate a state of being to you. What you think and how you experience the world and yourself communicates itself to your body. There is always dialogue between physical body and the other parts of self, as there is always communication between body and environment. For your body to be truly healthy, that dialogue needs to be restructured and investigated.

Take the time to experience yourself as healed. Use all of your senses to reorient yourself to being fully in your own body, environment, and experience. It is often helpful to have a ritual that signals to you that the healing is complete and your energy is now fully engaged within. You can wash your hands or shake them out. Have a phrase or mantra of your own that you say a few times, or any type of signal to yourself that it is time for your attention to shift back to taking care of you.

How to Do a Healing Session on Someone Else

First, you must create a space for healing. The function of this space is to give your subject a sense of safety and to give yourself enough protection so that your focus is on your subject. If you can, create a physical space; if you simply can't, create a psychological space by expressing the intention to engage in a healing and letting nothing around you get in the way.

Let the subject know how long you will be working with her and stick to that time. This will create a framework for both of you, so that you use the time effectively. I always let my client know what I am *not*. I am not a doctor, I cannot make medical recommendations, I am not a therapist, and I cannot "process" the material that comes up with clients. I instead let them know what I *am*. I use energy to try to impact their energy in a healing way. I am an intuitive. I will be giving them my intuitive impressions of what is going on and what is changing during the healing. I also tell them that some of this may be incorrect and that they should believe themselves first and foremost. They may have memories, feelings, and experiences during the healing that will be their own energy's way of working things out. The best way to use this effectively is for them simply to allow it to happen, not try to remember it, and not try to assist the process. What they need to remember they will remember, and what needs to retreat into the subconscious, they will again have access to when it is useful for them.

You can ask the subject what she wants to work on with you. Often the presenting complaint is neither the real issue nor what needs to be healed. Someone may say she wants to heal her asthma, but when you allow intuition to guide you it takes you to her unexpressed grief, which is suffocating any sense of happiness or pleasure in her life. I listen to my intuition first and foremost.

Tell your subject the physical process of what will be happening in the session. If you intend to touch your client or verbally share your intuitive information, ask her permission to do so. Assure her that she already knows her own information even if she is not conscious of it, and explain to her that if something you say feels wrong, it probably is.

The best position of attention for a subject is one where she doesn't have to do or change anything. Think about it: if she could heal herself, she wouldn't be asking you for a healing to begin with. Let her know that she doesn't have to do anything or remember anything. Give her permission to allow her mind to do, think, and wander wherever it naturally goes. She can't effectively do anything else anyway, so take the futile effort out of the mix. Let her know that you will be guiding the session and that she can't do anything to get in the way or to make it more effective, although you will give her some things to do at home after the session.

You need to be in control of the session. Unless you are a psychotherapist and you want to integrate therapy into the healing, it is best to avoid conversation with your subject during the healing. Chances are the conversation will be your subject's way of derailing or taking control of the healing. If your subject is in control, she will maintain the dysfunctional status quo. Let her know that you will be happy to discuss anything after the healing is over.

I often like the subject to close her eyes, as it takes the necessity of interacting with her out of the equation. Your attention during the healing will be on perceiving and changing her energy, as well as receiving intuitive information to catalyze a reaction within her. You don't need to divide your attention even further by having to be present in a social, interactive way.

Do whatever preparation you find effective to focus your

energy. Remember to give yourself the suggestion that as you run energy through her, you will first be attending to healing yourself.

Begin by placing your attention or your hands on your client. Notice where you choose to begin. You will immediately have a sense of how the area needs to change in order to heal. You will most likely get a sense of what the dysfunction is and what the energy would be like if it were healthy. Use your attention and your breath to force that change. This is a different process for everyone. You may see it, feel it, or engage any combination of senses to perceive the problem and the relevant solution. At the periphery of your attention you will notice scenes, words, and ideas that will address what is going on in that area or catalyze a change. Unless your information seems really cruel or unethical (like suggesting that she stop her medication), report it to your subject. If there is something that she needs to change or do differently or even attract into her life, do it for her. It is really unhelpful to say to a subject, "I see that you are lonely." Your job as a healer is to help her address that. If you perceive that she is lonely, you also need to perceive the energetic solution, and perhaps support your conclusions with some history so she doesn't feel like you are just making it up or, worse, pouring salt into her wounds.

For example, you might say: "I sense loneliness in your left lung." (She may know she has a lesion there, and you may see it as well, but not being a doctor and being ethical, you don't give medical information. If she doesn't know it is there, she will be alerted to check it out. "I feel you in the middle of many kids, maybe siblings, and a sense of being forgotten. In your present life I sense that you are so used to being overlooked that you don't know how to draw people toward you. I am changing that dynamic now. I am drawing good people to you and experiencing you mirroring their healthy behavior and making positive relationships, and as I do this I feel anger coming up. I am sensing you becoming more physically active so that the anger doesn't stop your nascent ability to create connection. Now I am drawn to your belly . . ."

You will find that once you begin the healing your attention will know where to start and then, moment to moment, where to go next. You are energetically creating a map of healing in your subject. Remember, people do not live in a vacuum. While you are healing your subject, also allow your attention to do the same for the dysfunctional situations that you perceive in her life. You cannot separate a body from its environment. You need to work on both.

When the time is up, stop, even if you feel like continuing. Tell the client to rest for a moment.

How to Conduct a Remote Healing Session

Now we are going to do the same exercise remotely on someone else or on yourself, as if you were another person. This time you will not use your hands but simply hold an awareness of the other person in front of you (you can make his body bigger or smaller to suit your comfort). Remember to use the energy first to heal your own body, and then, with what we call the mind's eye, place your attention on the area of his body where you are drawn to begin the healing process. You may get a very clear sense of what you want to change in his body; you may experience cells working in a healthy way, their energy released to function in the most perfect manner for that person. You may have to keep pretending in order to do this. If so, make it the effort of your imagination.

You may find your attention moving to different parts of his body. You may find yourself speaking to him in your head, your intuition providing the exact words, images, and feelings that are needed to create a healing reaction. Let's finish up now by putting your attention once again on your own body and allowing the energy to focus on your healing. You may be very surprised by the accuracy and clarity of your intuitive impressions of what is going on with the other person. One of my greatest joys as a teacher of healing is seeing my students' surprise when they realize that even from a distance they were accurate about what was going on with another person and were able to have a positive effect.

If you're in contact with your subject, tell your subject the healing is done. There can be time for sharing, or you can simply let him have a moment to take notes on what he heard from you or perceived in himself. You will most likely have some areas of suggestion for him to focus on after the healing that would be helpful to share with him.

As you get more practiced at this technique you will become very directed in how your intuition tells you to change the energy of the body (and all that is attached to it), and your intention will be clear from the outset.

Healing Yourself First

As you read in the last few examples I outlined, it's important first to use energy to heal yourself. One of the wonderful functions of a healthy subconscious is that it will not allow you to give away something without somehow also addressing your own wishes and needs. If you use the process of giving a healing to also heal yourself, your subconscious will give you a much greater access to energy, because you are doing the healthy and natural thing of taking care of yourself first. That is why you embody *you* before you do a healing. Healers who say that they are exhausted by doing a healing or picking up symptoms from their clients are not taking this very important and effective first step of using every interaction to also heal themselves. The only psychic, psychological, and physical self-defense is to fully inhabit you.

The body is a complete and highly complex system, and in many ways it is harder to heal than a company or a relationship, as you have to work against a lifetime of patterns, many of which you are no longer conscious of, if you ever were! Healing yourself is a brave task. There is no perspective when you work on yourself. More than any other intuitive skill, healing is the one where I will most often ask someone else to perform it on me. We all tend to avoid our Achilles' heels. We don't instinctively poke at the place that hurts—yet that is precisely what is usually needed for healing.

I'm sure you know how you feel when you feel good. You experience your best possible interpretation of reality and a strong sense of a positive and fulfilled destiny. If you cannot find that place in yourself in this moment, find a single, powerful memory when you were feeling your best and all was right with your world. In this memory, all of your senses, including your thinking, judgment, and outlook, your taste, smell, feeling, hearing, and sight were filled; you were flooded in a visceral, sensory way with total well-being. Every atom of your being was fully alive.

You were composed of and filled with the best possible you. This is your starting point for a healing. This in and of itself is a healing technique that you can use on yourself at any time. It is good to have a memory catalog from which you can choose your state of being. Why memory? Memory, you see, already exists in a complete form, so you can always refer to it. You don't have to imagine it or create it, and intuition can pick and choose its best parts and fill in the blanks to make it even more alive and complete. You need to find that state.

Embody your own healing. Experience it with all of your senses. This will not be easy. The first thing that you are aware of when you embody and fully experience something that you are struggling to create are the blocks to its creation. Once you are conscious of a block, you can begin to use it as a tool. Often your intuitive healing can give you a more complete and wonderful result than you could ever visualize, as you may never have experienced this state of well-being, love, success, health, or happiness before.

Healing Techniques You Can Use in Your Daily Life

I strongly suggest that you create a physical healing space. I have a few healing spaces in my house, starting with my couch, where I work with others, and my bed, where I work on myself. I like using my bed as my healing space as it sets me up to be ready to heal during the night's sleep as well. Next to my bed I also have a small cushion and table with meaningful healing items—photos of loved ones, small mementos, and gifts. I make sure to change them and move them around as my life heals and moves. Your healing space should be responsive to your changes, and if you are practicing healing, those changes may happen quickly.

I have a little box of healing items that I travel with, and I set up a healing space wherever I go. This reminds my subconscious, "This is your space for healing and regeneration." It is essential to have something outside of yourself to document, represent, and pattern your internal changes. Inside of you things are messy and enmeshed. When you create an outer space that represents and follows your changes, you are able to experience those changes and implement them more clearly. There are so many ways to do this. I used to love making a diorama (you know, the shoe box in which you create a little world) of what I wanted. All through school I made dioramas of the home I wanted, and now I live in it! Put the effort into making your external space resemble exactly what it is you want to heal and create. Listen to your excuses as to why you can't do this: "I live with other people," "I have no money," and "I don't have time." These are the excuses you use to stay stuck. Use what you have, start from where you are, and you will be amazed at what you will create and how that will translate into your real life in a powerful and satisfying way.

You may also want to have a healing space that you go to in your imagination. It should engage all of your senses and in some way resemble the healing space you have created in your home, some kind of internal, portable healing space that you can always carry with you. This is the place where you heal. You may heal simply by walking through its door, if it has a door. There may be a large Roman bath where you submerge yourself in healing waters. You may have an all-powerful, all-loving healing being who holds you. As long as all of your senses are engaged in this inner healing place, it will be a powerful intuitive, physical, emotional, and spiritual destination of regeneration and re-creation for you. Having taught this work for quite a long time now, I will let you in on a funny little secret: all your spaces—your home, office, and car—will begin to resemble your healing spaces over time. You may also intuitively seek out countries, hotels, and restaurants that resemble your healing spaces. Most important, you will attract a life that makes you feel how you feel when you are in the process of healing.

How to Rejuvenate Yourself

This one is everybody's favorite healing (everyone over the age of thirty, that is). Rejuvenation may seem shallow, but rejuvenation is one of the most powerful healing tools that we have. Your energy has memory. Your cells have memory. Memory isn't permanent. It can be changed with a variety of techniques.

Go back to a time of optimal health or development. In the case of wanting to feel rejuvenated, simply take your cells and your energy back to that place; in the case of illnesses that are genetic, or that happened at birth, or when you were far younger than an age you would like to return to, revise what the body did at that time, and then slowly forward the revised version of physical-emotional-intellectual self to the age you want it to be. Think of it as self-engineered inner cloning.

To instruct your cells toward youth, you must see yourself as young when you look into a mirror. This is, as all healing is, a process, a discipline. You need to use all of your senses, including sight, which with rejuvenation is often the hardest to employ. It may not be exactly as you were when you were young. You need to get the youth vision first and then edit. Perhaps there are things about your body you never liked and would like to edit in the vision. Perhaps in the period of time when you thought you looked your best, there was an illness or an emotional state that you want to release before your energy mimics this time period. This information will be apparent to you as you do the work. The gift and the curse of intuition are that the longer you are aware of something, the more information you receive. As long as you have a conscious target or goal, this information will help you reach it.

Similarly, if you are working to help someone else achieve rejuvenation, allow intuition to give you a sense of her perfected younger state and describe it to her, asking her to experience it with all of her senses and become part of the process by reporting to you what feelings, memories, and senses become highlighted for her as you work, as well as the things that she would like to change about her physical-emotional being from that time. Energy, cells, and atoms are very good at taking direction. When you give them a conscious direction, which often takes repetition and therefore the engagement of your subject in the process, they follow the prescribed direction. It is all about having the right language with which to give direction. You are too fat, you are too old, you are (fill in the blank) is *not* the right direction. Use your own intuition to bathe the truth in gentle terms.

The Do-Over:
Healing the Heart and Soul

In your mind's eye allow yourself to wander back to a younger you who needed all that you are right now to make yourself safe. Find a single scene. Place yourself with that child who was you and comfort her, tell her what she needs to know, try to make friends with her, to acquire her trust. Feel your love for her. If this is difficult for you, work to find what you could love about her, and let it grow. Every day do another scene. Only do this once, at most twice a day. As you heal the you of the past, you will also heal your present. The only rule is that you cannot change the past, only your response to it—what you did, felt, believed, said, and knew. You can bring your child home with you for a bit. You can tuck her into your life now. If you let her down by not fulfilling some of her dreams, you can work together to come up with a plan to make those dreams happen today. You are the best of allies.

Allow your awareness to move to a part of your body and follow it. Where did it go? What did you find there? What memories, abilities, and awareness are now clear and accessible for you to work with? Sometimes, the awareness alone is enough to begin the process of healing.

How to Lose Weight from Your Couch

Although this may seem an incredible concept, as far as I am concerned, so are diets. If diets and diet books worked, there would not be a multi-multibillion-dollar diet industry. You can and will experience how you can address your body in a new and effective way. If weight is an issue for you, it is a symptom of how you want to change your life. By changing your weight you will change your life.

Intuition is an amazing tool for weight loss because it guides you to the right choices for you, as a unique individual, as well as addressing the physical and psychological reasons that you, as an individual, are blocking yourself from having the body you want. Many of these reasons were helpful to you once, but now, just by choosing to read this, you are clear that they are no longer helping you. You are ready for change.

When you look at any human body, even identical twins, you find that no two bodies are the same. No two people are the same. Intuition will guide you to find what you need, specifically, accurately, and effectively for your own unique shape. It will also guide you to the resources that are right for you. You will guide yourself to good choices. The irony is that I won't be speaking a lot about diets and food, exercise, or any of those things that you would expect. You will be making deep, inner changes in yourself that will guide you to success. I know that many of you have really suffered from effort after effort, sacrifice after sacrifice, only to find yourself failing to live in the body that you want. Part of what you need to purge right now is the suffering, the shame, the self-loathing that failure brings. You tried. This is in itself a courageous act. Change, any change, is seen as a threat by all mammals. It requires new skills and a letting go of something that defines us and has helped us survive in the past. It is like a little death. Honor yourself for your effort toward change as you embark on real, sustainable change. The most valuable result of doing this program will not be weight loss—that will be just a side effect of the other changes you will be making. The treasure is the power, joy, and effectiveness you will gain in reclaiming yourself and the ability to create your own life and your own destiny. I have never known anyone who, when they really found the core of their being, did not fall madly, passionately in love with themselves.

I am going to get the diet recommendations over with, right here and now. The simple truth is that when you ingest fewer calories than you expend, you lose weight. When you ingest more calories than you expend, you gain weight. Period. Many underlying conditions such as depression or anxiety can have an effect on your energy level, and as a result your weight. You may find yourself guided to have these conditions treated by a doctor. Of course, genetics play a part in how we gain or lose weight; however, you may find that by changing the way you use your energy, you change the way your brain works. I know many formerly obese people from obese families who have addressed their genetic tendencies in a way that yielded excellent results. You are the only powerful force of change in your life. You can change now.

On New Year's Day, many of us set ourselves up for failure. We decide to change things that we have failed to change in the past, all at once. Of course we just doom ourselves to more failure. Willpower only works when we can uncover and free our will. We will be doing this together, and in freeing your will you will free yourself from so many things you no longer need to carry around, one of them being excess weight. But I am sure that there are many more important and exciting things that will come to you in the process.

Remember that fat is stored energy, so transform it into useful energy. It is trying to protect you. It knows how you will protect yourself when it is gone. Let it know what you are going to use the energy for.

Reclaiming the Body You Were Meant to Have

This is an exercise in claiming yourself and your life so thoroughly that all areas find a new structure, one that is natural and desired by you. Intuition will allow you to guide yourself to your own unique and appropriate method of living and changing. If your way of conducting your life is no longer getting you the results you want, chances are that you are stuck in an outmoded, defensive style. At some point in your life the defense and the sacrifices you made to maintain it served you, may even have saved your life, but now you have other choices. The first and greatest element in change is choice, and the greatest tool of change is awareness.

Let us begin. You can do this exercise while sitting, while listening to music, or even washing dishes. There is no right way to do this. Right now I want you to experience your body exactly the way you want it to be. Don't visualize and don't use an idea of someone else's body that you admire. Pretend that you are a sculptor, and using the clay of your own body, as you inhabit it, create the body you want. As you do this, use all of your senses as your tools. How does it feel, taste, smell, sound, look to be in your body? What has changed inside of you? How do you feel about yourself and the world around you? You don't have to focus or make a big process of doing this. Remember, you can be doing something else at the same time.

What will happen is that all of the things in your life—your thoughts, your body, your history, and your patterns that don't allow you to be in this new body—will come to your awareness. This will not happen all at once, but in layers. Notice these things (you may even want to write them down), and then go back to sculpting. You may even want to take this new body for a test drive, moving around the room in it. You don't need to block the negative observations or messages about your body that may come up as you do this. Notice them, go back to sculpting, and breathe. You may find that emotions come up for you, or that people or situations come to mind. Bring your focus back to sculpting your body from the inside out. The longer that you can stay with this exercise in attention, the more powerfully you can make a profound change. The interference, the judgment, the despair, and the anger are all part of the process; they are not distractions but instead are all part of changing the pattern of energy that has kept you trapped where you no longer want to be.

Continue to move from your distractions back to your sculpting. The *you* who you no longer want to be is not the overweight you; there is so much more to it. The weight is just a symptom, and as you continue to sculpt and allow yourself to be aware of the other distracting information, bringing yourself back again and again to the you that you are creating now, you master fully inhabiting the life you want and uncover the skills within you to do so.

How to Heal a Situation
in Your Life

You can hold the whole situation between your hands, allowing it to progress in time or allowing its details to change to promote healing. You can hold yourself, at that time, in your hands, and in your mind's eye guide your younger self to safety. Your intuition, once you begin a healing, will give you numerous original and pertinent ways to create positive change.

Often you will have to do this more than once. I suggest that after the healing you take notes on what you experienced, or if you are not a writer, draw, sculpt, or pursue some other creative outlet that will document the experience for you. You will often need to sleep after you do this kind of healing on yourself. Your subconscious and senses will want downtime to process the information and integrate the energetic changes you have made.

Using Healing in Your
Day-to-Day World

Healing is a focus of energy and attention that gives you a powerful ability to direct not only what is happening inside of you, but also what is happening around you. If you want to raise money for your company, you use your telepathy and mediumship to find out what investors would respond to; your embodiment to experience yourself and your product as the desired person or group; your remote viewing to direct you to investors; and your body heat to draw them to you. It is your *healing*, your taking in of all of the data and energy and focusing it on the desired outcome, that creates the pattern that quickly draws the pieces into place. And I am here to tell you that you can literally do this the easy way, sitting on your couch. Hold the desired outcome between your hands, breathe and allow all of your intuitive skills to give you information, all of the time using your breath and your attention to repattern and reset all the diverse elements that would let you achieve your goal. In fact, you can create success and then just walk into what you need. The work, the hard work, is done on your couch, consistently and with discipline.

I use a rather stupid but effective process when healing gives me so much intuitive work to do. Dumbing it down helps me to navigate to my goal when it seems as if I am trying to negotiate an obstacle course. Here goes: I experience my goal as a gumball (any color will do) in a sphere of other multicolored gumballs, and I keep my attention, my breath, and my energy on pushing my gumball through the rest until it is where I want it to be (I often don't quite know the destination until I get there and perceive it with my remote viewing). On the way, I encounter obstacles, which, if necessary, are defined by my intuition, along with ways of dealing with them. Sometimes the telepathic negotiation takes place below my awareness, and after a moment I can feel my gumball move forward. Sometimes my gumball slows or loses its bearings on its own, and then I can often feel, within my own body, why this is happening, and I dialogue with myself or use intuition to find the tools and reassurances that will allow me to feel empowered to move forward. I do this until my goal is met—until my gumball gets to where it needs to go.

Here is an example. I love teaching and I want to do more of it when my son goes to college. To feel good about being a teacher, however, I have to be able to set my students up with the kind of practice that will support them and empower them in the world. Seemingly out of the blue, and right before the Big Crash of 2008, as it will come to be known, *Newsweek* calls me to do an article on my work. The article focuses on business and intuition. The same month I make a market prediction (I never do this, *ever*) on the radio about oil prices, and the price of oil obliges; then, just to top it off, the fact that I predicted this market crash for many of my clients is made public by one of them, and instantly I have skilled, educated students to train and a market of people who want to hire the business intuitives whom I have trained.

Of course, the reverse could have been true. If I were directing my energy through my introversion, which I battle with, I could have drawn to myself a reporter who would have found my mistakes, and I would have been rewarded by being left alone. This is the flip side of healing at work, and the reason why it is so important to have your subconscious and its injuries on board, heard, and dealt with and your healing directed consciously toward your goals. This is true of a person, a company, a community, a situation, and so on.

Intuition and observation give you plenty of data. The complex and dynamic process of directing what we know, what is available through the inner and outer roadblocks to end up at the goal, is healing. Everyone you work with needs to be able to do this or they become a roadblock in and of themselves. You do not have to use psychic language, and in fact, you probably shouldn't. Use words like *focus* and questions such as, "Are you taking care of yourself in this?" "What are your reservations?" "What are the potential difficulties, and "How can we come together to resolve them?" Normal directions and questions placed correctly engage intuitive and healing responses.

There is an old psychotherapy game called "elephant." Everyone is on their hands and knees blindfolded on an obstacle course. Only the leader can see. It is the leader's job to take everyone to the finish line safely and the rest of the group's job to cooperate with those ahead and those behind in following the leader to the goal. At the beginning of the exercise everyone is a bit haphazard. By the end, each person in the line is part of the leader, adding power and energy to the progression. You can do this with your family or your company without getting on your hands and knees. It is incredibly therapeutic. Healing takes energy from disorganized, adversarial, and dysfunctional patterns and channels it, using the very energy that would have impeded your progress, as fuel for reaching your goal.

Healing Is a Process

You may be wondering, with all of these positive healing changes in your life and the good fortune they bring to you in the world, why would you ever not practice healing? Why would you ever go back to old habits or be distracted from your most joyful and powerful path? But you will be, over and over again, and good old discipline will have to take up the slack. Why will this happen? Very simple: because life intervenes. Other people's demands and the basic demands of life will distract you. Old reactions to friends, coworkers, and even to memories will lure you away. The subconscious is suspicious of change and will try to engage you in whatever it needs to keep you the same, to keep you stuck. Change means a loss of the old self, and no matter how badly you may feel about an illness or an image of yourself, it is you, and you have cared for it and put a lot of energy and time every day in keeping it the same. It takes discipline and courage at some point in the process of healing to allow for real change. One of my other books, *Welcome to Your Crisis,* can help you avoid the pitfalls of your reactive style, and help you recognize how to extricate yourself when you fall back, using the strengths of your style to move you forward.

Sometimes at the beginning of a healing you don't really know what your goal is. If you are doing a healing on others, their initial goals or "presenting complaints" may not be what really needs to be healed. Healing is a continuous process of discovery and change; it is organic and evergreen. No one, nothing, is ever fully healed. Everything is a dynamic, ever-growing work in progress. The moment you transform one thing, you work on the next level of health, happiness, and success. You can learn to love the gradual unveiling of your best ally and friend—*you.* Consistency is key to healing your own life. It took time to create the patterns that don't work, and it will take time and consistency to replace them with ones that do.

Healing rarely follows a methodical and logical progression. Think of your whole self as a circle made up of many points, all of which are interconnected. You may jump around from point to point—symptom to memory to feeling to previously undiscovered ability, back to feeling, to a piece of good fortune you allow into your life, to memory and so on—until you have connected the dots and drawn yourself a circle of completeness. In math, if a polygon (a multisided, closed object, just as we are in our conscious life) has infinite sides, it becomes a circle. All of the sides of an issue, reflecting their images in different directions, become life's most perfect and infinite shape, a circle, when merged with the infinite understanding and potential of intuition.

As you become a healer, of yourself as well as of others, you will feel your connection and your access to the strength and power of all that is around you. You will feel the mobility of the past, your ability to create the future, and be aware and responsible for the choices you make in action, attention, and intention in the present. It is in the present that you can change it all. Healing is best reflected in Voltaire's quote from the ancient philosopher Timaeus of Locris on the image of god: "A circle whose centre is everywhere and circumference nowhere." In the experience of the limitless circumference of your own being, you find your healing as you bring that infinite good back to your own center. You can do this now.

Healing Raises Blocks and Other Issues

As with every technique in this book, your belief is not required for the techniques of healing to succeed. However, if you do not document your desired goals or outcomes you will have no way of testing whether or not you were able to create change. If you do not allow yourself to prove this very effective tool to yourself, it will be hard for you to invest energy into using it.

It is never helpful to disempower what someone is already doing. Belief is a powerful tool when it comes to healing. It allows the subconscious, the master control, to get on board. It is not necessary to create the healing, but it is necessary to sustain it or the subconscious will simply build up new dysfunctional patterns. If you (or someone you are practicing on) believes that your megadose of vitamin C will help, or your chemo or a skin product will enhance your chances of a cure, your very belief may be what creates its usefulness. Be careful of how you tread on your own and others' healing beliefs. Be aware of your own bias so that you do not impose it on your client or target, and do the hard work to question your beliefs in yourself. A belief is a lovely thing because you accept it without question. However, there are many beliefs that you hold that may be affecting every area of your life negatively. These beliefs need to be questioned and refined for you to heal your life.

What if the healing is not working? Can you heal someone or something that does not want to be healed, and is it right to do so?

Volition is an important part of healing. If something is not transforming, there may be a deep and persistent reason why you are afraid, why you reject, and why you resist what you will have to do in order to change or what you will have to acknowledge for the healing. This is true of a person, a company, society at large, and even the world. There may be a reason why enduring the symptom is less painful than recognizing its source. Maybe confronting how your father really felt about you is more painful than your illness. Maybe being alone is less painful than looking at your own rage or fear. We make choices every day about which pain we choose to deal with. Remember, the subconscious is *sub*-conscious. All we can do is work consistently and persistently to bring our subconscious beliefs and patterns to the direction of consciousness (even if it is in the dream state and only semiconscious), where the energy can be released and redirected for desired change.

One of the greatest impediments to healing is the inability of yourself or of your subject to experience where you or they are right now. Well, the reality is that if you are in crisis you are already there, and the energy spent on pretending that you are not is better spent on creating what you want. Whatever it is that is blinding you to what is really going on for you right now is also blinding you to its resolution. It takes an enormous amount of courage to really perceive our own lives as they are in this moment. In order to have this courage you have to be able to, at the very least, entertain the idea that you—*you*—have the power to change.

Self-help is just that. It is the ability to find the power within yourself and your connection to the world to help yourself. I am very opposed to gurus. One of the best compliments I ever received from a student was, "Wow, you are really screwed up and your life still works great." The point is that we are all works in progress. You are your own best guru. Those who have traveled the path before you can give you the map, but you will find the best way to create the journey for yourself. Perfect beings have nothing to teach you. Embrace where you are right now. Whatever is going on with you, no matter how devastating it may be, is happening to help you find your most powerful self.

You are where you are and who you are in this moment. The next moment is yours to create, but only if you have the courage to embrace what this moment is for you now and who you are, what you are experiencing in the present moment. The way to ignite this is by starting with the statement "I have the power to change," and then feel that statement with all of your senses. Then you are ready to look at where you are and what you need to change.

Healing is bringing something to a higher and more productive level of functioning, and often it is confrontational and, well, uncomfortable. In healing you uncover and clean the abscesses that left untended will poison the system. It is ugly but it works. You are directing energy to change an established pattern of energy. You will rarely be greeted with a welcome mat, at least at first.

I joke that my five-day students hate me for two days and then love me for the next three. I poke, prod, anger, and sometimes even bore with repetition. I do everything I can to bring people's symptoms to the surface, and they hate me for it. I get some of the most vicious feedback I have ever seen from second-day workshop dropouts, and there are many. By day five the response forms are so loving and grateful, and the people who write them are part of my life for the rest of my life.

Healing is about overpowering a dysfunction. On some level, every dysfunction has a purpose and is protecting itself, unwilling to heal. A practiced healer skillfully outwits, overpowers, and redirects the energy of dysfunction. Guess what? This is what makes a good CEO! You do not need the target's conscious cooperation to heal it. You actually need to assume that the cooperation will not be there, since in healing the first thing to be revealed is usually the symptom. A fever rises to its highest just before it breaks.

So, the simple answer is that you do not need permission to heal a system or a person effectively. A dysfunction is usually weaker than the organized, directed, intuitively informed energy of a healer. Whether or not it is right to heal an addict at his wife's request is entirely up to the individual. Keep in mind that we are subconsciously using healing all of the time. Part of a solid morality is making conscious choices about how you use your energy.

Intuitive Healing Is Not a Replacement for Medical Professionals

Don't give up your doctor. Healing is part of getting your finances where you want them to be, but don't fire your accountant, either. In fact, a good accountant is part of the healing. Healing is a powerful and dynamic way to help yourself and others create dramatic change quickly. As a healer, whether of yourself or someone else, your goal is for the healing to occur. That means that anyone or anything that can aid in this process is also part of the healing. Sometimes the surgery is the healing. The medication is part of the healing. You may have to entertain the possibility that allopathic medicine can help you to heal even if it is against your belief system. Although you will be working on a technique that allows you to create physical healing, using anything that helps the process of healing is useful. Rigidity, the inability to adapt in a healthy way, causes illness in the first place. Sometimes there are cases of real physical injury. You get into an accident, for example, maybe break a bone. Even these seemingly random injuries have stories to tell you and your intuition and have power to impart. Often, as you work with intuition and the energy of the dysfunction changes with your redirection, you will also be guided to the right doctor, the right treatment to aid in resolving your physical problem, the right people and information to support your change. We live in an interconnected universe. When intuition is engaged, it works in many ways.

By the way, there is no such thing as "medical intuition." Medical intuition is simply intuition. Unless you are a doctor there is no difference between being a medical intuitive and simply an intuitive. The difference is in the target or questions. Intuition gives you accurate information about a target. If the target is a human body with a problem, intuition will give you information about what that problem is and how to resolve it. *Practicing medicine without a license is a felony.* You don't want to be bad felonious fake doctors, do you?

The following instructions are true whether you are working with someone else or performing healing on yourself. You can, in a nonalarmist way, ask your subject when her last checkup was and gently direct her to go to her doctor while helping to give her the language to describe her symptoms to get the correct tests. You can say things like, "I feel a lot of grief held in your breast, and that your grief needs to be addressed. It might be a good thing to let the grief know you care by having a mammogram and addressing the physical, letting it know that you will take care of it in every way." You can say, "I feel like your body is wanting some minerals. Have you considered going to a nutritionist?" If you work as a healer, you will acquire a long list of referrals—good doctors, psychiatrists, nutritionists, and so on.

Even though I will treat my illnesses with traditional medicine when healing doesn't work, I ask myself, Why do I have this bronchitis? What is it telling me? Who is it? Where else am I holding this pain in my body? What do I need to change, do, ask for, or come to terms with for it to teach me what it needs me to learn? How is this illness expressing itself in other areas in my life, business, relationships, and so on? Sometimes I can't respond immediately. However, with intuition, once you pose the question the answer comes in its time. Recently I had a respiratory virus, and you don't treat a virus with antibiotics; they have to run their course. I did my "healing thing" and got a clear message that I needed time for rest and for myself. I needed to be creative and work less, but I was in the middle of scheduled business travel and couldn't do what my body was asking me to do. Then I arrived home, still sick, and my son was starting school. The virus helped me pick up a secondary infection, but I still didn't feel I had time to go to a doctor or get rest, and, of course, I became sicker. Finally I was so depressed that I took an hour off to go to my psychiatrist. I said, "I am depressed, maybe I need an antidepressant." He said, "No, you need an antibiotic." I took it, slept for two days, and got better.

I had a student in my last workshop who really wanted to be in a relationship. She had been taking some antidepression medication for a few months; for the first time in her life, it worked very well with no side effects against the depression that she had endured her whole life. In fact, prior to this medication, her life and choices had been defined and dictated by her depression. Right before my workshop, where she came to work on bringing a relationship into her life, she went off her medication. Her rational mind told her that this was an act of faith in her ability to find this relationship. I suggested to her that perhaps this was her way of avoiding finding her relationship by once again making depression her issue. Do not throw out the baby with the bathwater when doing healing. There are many things that will help you heal. Use good judgment and good intuition to employ them all.

Making Self-Healing a Daily Process

As always, when you write down your target, you direct your intuition clearly and powerfully. When you awaken in the morning, take a moment to document your dreams, your state of mind, feelings, and physical sensations. What are the physical issues in your body you would like to change? What would you like to change about the way you feel in life and about yourself?

If these different issues could speak, what would they say? List the things you want to heal, and let them speak to you or give you images and memories that will help you be their healer. Only you have the information you need to heal yourself.

Here are important questions to ask yourself:

• What are the risks in healing?

• What could I lose?

• What frightens me about being healthy and whole?

• Does or did anyone in my family have similar issues to mine? If this is my way of identifying with that person, what exactly would I be identifying with?

• Whom do I need to speak to now to clear my energy and symptoms? Name the person and then on this page say what you need to say.

• How would I describe the healed me?

• What am I like?

• What is my life like?

• Who is my friend, lover?

• What is my relationship to my family?

• What is my relationship to my past?

Allow the healed you to speak to you, as you are right now. Become one with the healed you. Hold something that you carry or wear each day as you do this exercise. When you feel in need of healing during the day, touch this object to cue you back into the healing state.

I also like to get the healing energy between my hands and send energy to my beverages. You can do this as a group. Create healing water as a group and then have each person take some home. Everything is energy, so you can charge, shift, and empower the energy in everything you use or consume. I cook dinner for my family every night, even though they like takeout just as much, just so that I can put love and healing into the preparation of their food.

Preparation for Sleep Work

Healing does not have to be done consciously, in a meditative state. In fact, you will do it more consistently if you make it part of your normal bedtime routine, doing it as you wash your face, brush your teeth, shower, read, and engage in other bedtime activities.

As you prepare for sleep, allow each part of your body that you tend to experience its new state of being. For example, if you have decided to lose weight, notice, as you put on your pajamas (or take off your street clothes) how lithe and firm your body is. If you are working toward health, experience the water of your shower washing away all but the strongest, most functional cells of your body; as you brush your teeth experience all of the systems of your body as being strong and fresh. Don't just do this with one of your nighttime rituals, do it with all of them. Especially before sleep, you can instruct your subconscious and dreams to work for you if you consciously work in your new state of being before losing consciousness to sleep.

Of course, this will not be easy to do, especially in the beginning. You will have to consistently bring your senses back to your new state of being. You will find, however, that the more you do this, the more intuition will give you information that can help you create the changes you want as you follow your routines. You may begin to notice that certain foods, activities, or treatments are brought to consciousness during your routine. You may become more aware of memories that may have contributed to the problem or can contribute to the solution. You may find that your body remembers being an age where you were healthy, thin, happy, balanced, or whatever change you are trying to achieve. Memories are interesting healing tools, as they can often give us a complete experience that is real for us of what we want to achieve now for our bodies. I include emotions in physical healing as I (and many physicians) have observed that much of what we think of as painful emotional feeling is actually our brain, endocrine system, or discomfort from our body in a state of disease. Once again, without studying *Gray's Anatomy* (the book, not the TV show) to figure out which body system isn't functioning to its fullest, intuition will give you a solution. It may be as simple as breathing more fully or as complex as having your blood sugar checked to make sure you don't have diabetes. Whereas there are many confirmed reports of miraculous physical healing, it is essential to get proper medical care while you are creating your miracle. Sometimes the medicine *is* the miracle. Many of the most unhealthy people I know are stuck on the idea that they have to heal, lose weight, rejuvenate, or whatever they are trying to achieve in a certain way. The rigidity becomes the illness. Vegans get sick, and my grandfather, God bless him, lived to the age of ninety-nine on cigars, smoked fish, and pound cake. If you listen to your body's intuition and then try things out, verifying what works and what doesn't, you will find your own unique path to healing.

Experiencing yourself as healed does not mean denying what is wrong and leaving it untreated. It means doing all the responsible things (seeing your doctor, finding a good diet, exercising, avoiding sun, depending on what you are changing in your body) while maintaining the experience of you, healed.

It is a fallacy that you can only have one state of consciousness. In fact, people who use the powers of their being fully have developed the ability to maintain contradictory feelings and experiences in their consciousness without being in conflict. The ability to do this allows the fullness of who you are, along with your being, to negotiate a better state of togetherness. There is wisdom in illness, aging, and dysfunction. They are trying to tell you something that you need to respond to for your happiness and well-being to emerge. Its message should not be dissipated before it is learned; however, insisting on the healed state will speed this process and help your body to reveal its wisdom to you more clearly and readily.

A Final Thought as
You Go on to Rule the World
from Your Couch . . .

I am sure that if you have trained with this book, you are now comfortable with your own ability to gain reliable information using your intuition. You may also have discovered how wonderfully freeing it is to be able to travel to, negotiate with, and experience anyone, any place, any situation, and any time with your intuition. You will find that as you use these techniques and processes consistently, you will also start to individualize them for your personal attention style and to meet the needs of your family, clients, company, or projects.

I used to love history class. The teacher would give me my target—ancient Rome, for example—and I would go there, eat the food, smell the air, and know the people. It is no coincidence that my Rome apartment is in the dormitory zone of the ancient centurions. They are old friends. As I walk the streets I walk through thousands of years of perceptions.

The development of any part of yourself—emotions, intellect, intuition, relationships, and your ability to create success in the world—enriches every atom of your being in a way that is beyond words. I sincerely hope that along with some new tools for success in your life, you have also found the pleasure of your own extended perceptions. At age twenty everything I did was for a goal, no matter what the cost, and the goal was what counted. At age fifty my goal is the joy. The love.

Keep training. You will have times, as I do, when intuition goes a bit south, often because you are struggling, bravely, with some new issue in your life. It is in these times when you need this book the most. The discipline and rigor of a methodical practice will put you back on track every time. I use this book, as well as *Welcome to Your Crisis* and *The Circle,* every day. Even though I wrote these books, I need to return to their pages to bring order to my own process. Life is overwhelming at times and a system cures confusion. I love to decoupage visual imagery on the covers or inside covers of my books so that I can engage sight in cuing my subconscious and intuition to my goals. I often scent my books and put them where I will see them, along with my journal, in my healing space.

I hate to sound like a self-help author, but *life is never perfect* and *life is always perfect.* Use what you have now, suspending judgment, and set your targets on what you want to create. One of my dearest friends was very successful and then went bust early in his career. What makes him so successful now is that he learned how to recover from his own fallibility and deal with the unreliability of the world around him at such a young age. It has also made him a very wise, intuitive, and wealthy (in money, friends, and family) young man.

I think my Achilles' heel was that I clung to control and perfection for too long. I got myself stuck. It took quite a few big live knockdowns to teach me that failing is often the stimulus for something new and better. We don't let go easily (see *Welcome to Your Crisis*), even *and especially* of the bad things.

Intuition will help you control and predict the world around you and get where you think you want to go far more quickly and with fewer mistakes. Take the time, however, to enjoy the weaknesses, the vulnerabilities, the "failures" that create the space for you to arrive at a success that you cannot even imagine in this moment. There is a time to lead, know, direct, and acquire and a time to let go, to allow your intuition to go on automatic pilot, keeping you safe while ceding control long enough to find yourself in new territory that you might have been too patterned, afraid, or content to approach otherwise.

I try to keep my beliefs out of my writing and stick to what works. But here for my fiftieth birthday I will give myself the gift of sharing one belief with you, one that has proven to be true for me whether I am using it to make a company competitive or to give where I would rather take:

We are all one energy.
Your success is mine and mine is yours.
Everything I write is simply a part of yourself that
you are now willing to hear.

I love your emails and your intuitions. Please get in touch at www.practicalintuition.com and healingday@aol.com.

I am the only one who reads my mail. They are our private communications. I treasure them.

With love,
Laura Day

Acknowledgments

First and foremost, this book is my legacy to you, my readers. Now you will be able to do what your companies hire me to do! I am going to have to find a new day job. Your demand for a linear explanation for a nonlinear process made me dissect the gift of intuition and write this book. Thank you for your questions, complaints, emails, and for sharing your stories and your lives with me.

Second, I am blessed with devoted, funny, delightful friends, many of whom I work with. I call the first bunch my three magic J's: Johanna, Judith, and Jennifer.

Johanna Castillo has made the editing of this book, dare I say, fun! You always show up in every way. Thank you for your . . . you.

Judith Curr, my publisher, is one of my favorite intuitives who knows the way to make everything happen just as it should. Thank you.

My friend, agent, and supreme commander, Jennifer Rudolph Walsh: how did I run my life without you? You have seen me through, well, perhaps it is TMI for the reader, but even my mother didn't follow me as closely as you do.

Margaret Riley, soon to rock the world: thank you for always patiently dealing with every bump in the road with efficiency, intelligence, and kindness and for making sure no one knows that I can't spell.

Dr. Frank Miller, one of the wisest, kindest men I know and my prototype for what to look for in a human being: there are no words to express my gratitude. So much of your wisdom is in this book and in all that I do.

David Globus, my father, for whom a ninety-eight on a test is a score missing two points: I could never have pulled rabbits out of a hat without you. I love you.

My mother, Vivian Globus, of blessed memory: You taught me to see the future and gave me the courage to live in the present. You live in my heart.

Thank you to so many people I have not mentioned here. I am blessed with my friendships. They sustain me in my dark moments and make the good times great. Thank you all.

A special thank-you to my son, my life's greatest blessing, now a man, who puts up with having to tell people his mother is an intuitive and who is now big enough to carry the heavy luggage. I love you. You are my sun.